History & Guide

WHICKHAM

Alan Brazendale

T0351187

History & Guide

WHICKHAM

Alan Brazendale

T

TEMPUS

First published in 2001

Reprinted 2008

Copyright © Alan Brazendale, 2001

Tempus Publishing, an imprint of
The History Press
Cirencester Road, Chalford, Stroud
Gloucestershire, GL6 8PE
www.thehistorypress.co.uk

ISBN 978 0 7524 2261 9

Typesetting and origination by
Tempus Publishing.
Printed and bound in Great Britain.

CONTENTS

PREFACE &

ACKNOWLEDGEMENTS

Whickham has changed dramatically over the last millennium. From being a farming community for many years, it was transformed, in the Middle Ages, into one of the most important coal-mining areas in the world, and then, as the mining industry declined, into its present existence as an attractive residential area renowned for its floral displays. In recent times, local councils (Gateshead nowadays, following Whickham and Tyne & Wear) have been at pains to remove the less attractive reminders of Whickham's industrial past while preserving and enhancing what was best. The centre of Whickham is a conservation area with many listed buildings, and in recent years reclamation sites to the east and west of Whickham have been transformed into attractive public recreation areas.

In some ways, this book has been in preparation since I first came to live in Whickham nearly forty years ago and it is impossible to thank everyone who has shared their memories and knowledge of Whickham history with me over that time. I must, however, again put on record my appreciation for all the assistance I have had from the staff of Gateshead Central Library, and in particular Eileen Carnaffin and Anthea Lang of the Local Studies Department, for their help with photographs and maps. I must also thank Mary Richardson, Development and Enterprise, Gateshead Council for information on Whickham Conservation Area and listed buildings, and Mr and Mrs Oloman of Park Cottage, Whickham, for lending me some of their unique collection of photographs. I hope they feel that this book repays their trust.

Alan Brazendale
November 2001

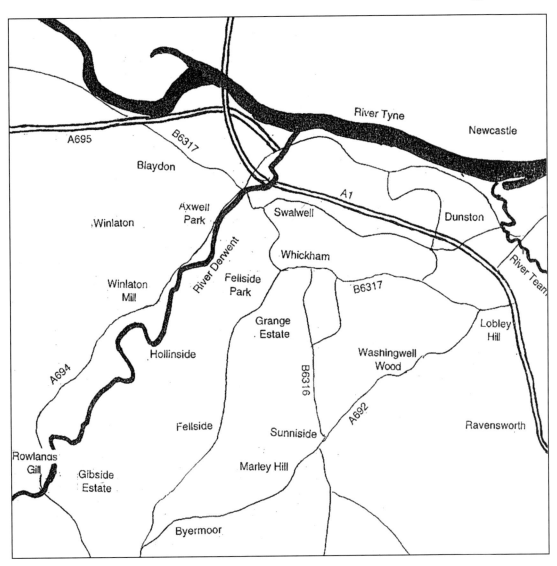

Outline map of the Whickham area.

CHAPTER 1

Whickham Through the Centuries

Whickham is situated at the northern end of a ridge of high land and is surrounded on three sides by rivers – the Tyne to the north, the Derwent on the west and the Team on the east – making it easily defensible, so it is not surprising that the site appears to have been occupied since prehistoric times. Artefacts which have come to light over the years include an axe, a beaker and an urn.

The name Whickham (or *Quykham* or *Qhickham*) has been used to refer to most of this area, between Team and Derwent, throughout history. The boundaries of Whickham Urban District Council, which was the local authority for the area prior to 1974, covered not only Whickham itself, but the substantial communities of Dunston and Swalwell situated where the Rivers Team and Derwent respectively joined the River Tyne, and the villages of Sunniside, Marley Hill and Byermoor to the south. Up to the second half of the nineteenth century, this area also formed a single Church of England parish until the growing population led to these various communities splitting away as separate parishes.

The origins of the name Whickham are uncertain. The 'ham' indicates that there was an Anglo-Saxon settlement on the site, but there are many alternative explanations for the prefix. In Anglo-Saxon '*wic*' means a village but 'wic-ham' would then mean something like 'village-village' which seems unlikely. '*Wicce*' means witch but there are no records of witchcraft being a particular problem in the area. 'Wick' means inland which could apply to many other settlements. The recent discovery of the site of a Roman fort has given rise to the suggestion that the prefix is derived from the Roman name for town '*vicus*' (the Romans pronounced *v* like a *w*) but this seems equally far-fetched. The likeliest explanation, which is now generally accepted, is that the original name was Quickham, as recorded in some early records, and that it described a settlement with a quickthorn hedge.

For much of its history Whickham seems to have been a simple farming community. From the fourteenth century onwards, however, the development of coal-mining became of increasing importance, and by the seventeenth century, Whickham was producing more coal per annum than any area of equal size anywhere in the world.

Indeed, a large proportion of the coal for which Newcastle became famous was actually mined in Whickham. Coal was still mined in the area until the second half of the twentieth century. It is those 600 years of coal-mining which have shaped much of Whickham's recorded history. Although Whickham contains many listed buildings, however, Gateshead Council, Whickham Council's successor, has made strenuous efforts to remove the less attractive physical remains of its industrial past, and it is difficult to visualise the industrial Whickham which used to exist in today's affluent residential area.

Roman Whickham

The sketch-map on the following page is based upon aerial photographs taken by Professor Norman McCord of Newcastle University while flying over Whickham in 1970 en route to photograph some known Roman sites. As the plane passed over Whickham, Professor McCord noticed crop markings in fields near Washingwell Wood and took historic photographs which showed the typical 'playing card' shape and the east and north gates of a Roman fort. Prior to this no one had suspected that there had been such a Roman presence in Whickham and the discovery led to a fundamental review of previous beliefs about the Roman frontier region. Up to the present time, the site has not been excavated, and many ideas about it must therefore remain pure speculation until further evidence comes to light. Unfortunately there is nothing to see at ground level and even from an aircraft, the crop markings are only visible in the right conditions and at certain

Aerial photograph taken by Professor Norman McCord in 1970 which first revealed the existence of Washingwell Roman fort.

Sketch map showing the location of Washingwell Roman fort.

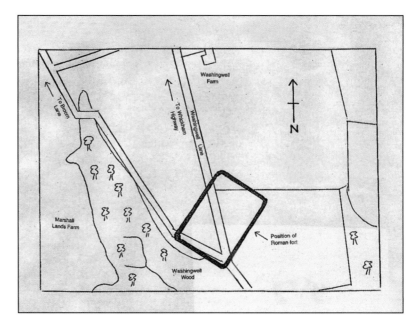

times of the year. The impact of the discovery of Washingwell fort on previous thinking about the Roman frontier is illustrated in the second sketch-map which shows the main features of the eastern end of the Roman frontier system before and after the discovery of Washingwell. A major puzzle had existed in relation to the Stanegate (i.e. 'stone road'). This was the road built between AD 78 and 84 which had formed the Roman frontier before Hadrian's Wall was built between AD 122 and the early 130s. The route of this road had been traced all the way from Carlisle to the east of Corbridge but had not been found between there and the east coast. Those seeking the Stanegate, however, had always made the assumption that it had run north of the Tyne like Hadrian's Wall. The discovery of Washingwell opened up the possibility that east of Corbridge the Stanegate had actually run south of the Tyne through Whickham and Wrekenton, and that the road known as the Wrekendyke was its eastern end. This possibility and the location of Washingwell fort are shown on the map as a broken line and open block. Bearing in mind that Hadrian's Wall had yet to be built, it must have seemed sensible in the first century AD to use the Tyne as a natural line of defence and to build the road behind it. The southward 'detour' which the road would have made through Whickham and Wrekenton and reason for it are illustrated in the third sketch-map. Until the 1930s, when the site was filled with colliery waste in the process of creating Team Valley Trading Estate, much off the lower end of Team Valley

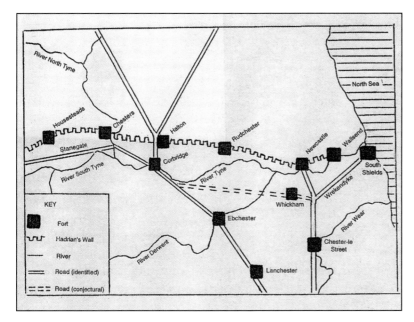

Sketch map illustrating the impact of the discovery of Washingwell fort on thinking about the Roman frontier.

was marshland. Indeed, there is some evidence that in Roman times the area was flooded at high tide. In these circumstances, it would be logical to route the Stanegate round the southern edge of the low-lying area with forts at Whickham and Wrekenton in commanding key positions.

There is, unfortunately, a strong probability that coal-mining and other industrial activity has destroyed much of the evidence which might have proved or disproved these theories.

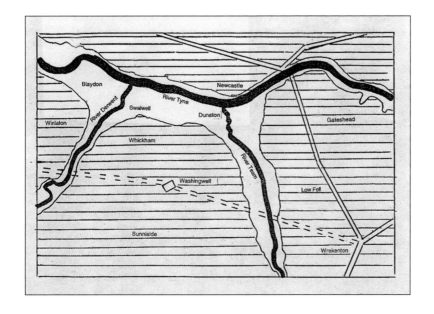

Sketch map illustrating why the Stanegate may have been routed to the south of the lower Team Valley area.

The Normans and After

While we really know nothing about the Romans' activities in Whickham, we know very little more about life in the village for several hundred years after their departure, and it is only with the advent of the Normans that we begin to have written historical records. Even then, Whickham lay in an area which was not covered by the *Domesday Book* because it was part of Durham at a time when Durham was a County Palatine where the king's authority was replaced by that of the all-powerful Bishop of Durham. No doubt Whickham was troubled for the century or so after the Norman Conquest by the ongoing wars with the Scots but we have no real evidence about this. However, in 1183, Bishop Pudsey called for a survey of his property which covered the whole of Durham with parts of Northumberland and Yorkshire, and it is as part of this survey, known as the *Boldon Book*, that Whickham's written history may be said to begin. At the time of the *Boldon Book*, the Bishop had thirty-five villein tenants (i.e. serfs) in Whickham, representing a total population of about 100 to 150 people, which would have been a fairly substantial community for the time. Each villein held an 'oxgang' or 'bovate' (as much land as a team of oxen could plough and make ready for sowing in a year) of 15 acres, but for this he had to pay a rent of 16d and do a considerable amount of unpaid work for his feudal lord, the Bishop. This included doing three days' work per week throughout the year (week-work) with extra work at ploughing and harvest times (boon-work). In addition to this, the community had to erect a cottage 40ft long and 15ft wide every year, serve in the Bishop's fishery, provide him with a hen and ten eggs per oxgang and a milch cow, and provide a cartage service for the Bishop's belongings between Durham, Gateshead and Bedlington when required. At that time there were two village officials. The Bishop's head man or grieve had a holding of 24 acres in recognition of his additional responsibilities. The *pinder*, who was responsible for rounding up stray cattle and holding them in the pinfold, also had land but in addition received a share of the harvest as payment for his duties. At the time of the *Boldon Book*, therefore, Whickham seems to have been a stable and, presumably, peaceful agricultural community. A hundred years later this peace was to be seriously disrupted.

The Fourteenth Century

Towards the end of the thirteenth century, Edward I's wars with the Scots began and these were subsequently carried on by his son

Edward II into the fourteenth century. The effect on Whickham was traumatic. In 1312 Edward II sent a writ to the Vicar of Whickham seeking 100s from him and a further £10 from the parish. A reply was sent saying that 'the goods of Quickham are wholly destroyed and carried away by the Scots'. Later in the same year a return of sequestered lands and goods in the diocese of Durham included Quickham to the value of 100s. In this case the reply stated that 'the sequestered goods we have not been able as yet to raise anything because we have not found purchasers on account of the fear of the Scotch, who a great part of the country thereabout have burnt and destroyed'. Two years later, in 1314, the bishopric contributed 1,500 men to the Battle of Bannockburn, many of them no doubt from Whickham. The defeat was followed by a disastrous famine in which, according to the *Annals of Whickham*, 'corn rose to an enormous price, and the miserable inhabitants of the villages fed on carrion and human flesh. In addition to these horrors, the Shevalds or mountain robbers continually plundered the diocese'. Later in the century, in 1348, the Black Death appeared for the first time with re-visitations in the 1350s and 1370s. There are no records of what happened in Whickham, but nationally the death toll ranged between 20 and 50 per cent of the population and there is no reason to think that Whickham was spared its share of the devastation. The fourteenth century was a black one for Whickham from every point of view. Two events are worthy of particular note, however, as indications of 'things to come'. The first event took place in 1343-44 when forty-one individuals, including the Mayor of Newcastle and three Newcastle bailiffs, were put on trial because, according to the *Annals of Whickham*, 'not being Bishop's officers, they had forcibly broken and cut the weirs in the River Tyne at Gateshead, Quickham and Ryton, and had taken away certain vessels laden with corn, coal, and other merchantize [*sic*] at Quickham, to unload without the liberty of the Bishop, and prevented vessels plying or unloading or bringing provisions or goods to Heworth-upon-Tyne, Hebburn, Jarrow, or Wyvestowe; and fisheman [*sic*] from bringing and selling fish there.' This appears to be the first of the series of battles between Newcastle and its southern neighbours to control commercial activities on and around the Tyne which was to last for centuries. The second important event occurred in 1356, when Bishop Bury granted a lease of the mines under the manors of Whickham and Gateshead, to Sir Thomas Grey, Kt, and John Pulhore, rector of Whickham, for 500 marks (£333 6s 8d) rent. If the rent should be in arrear at any time for forty days, the

amount was to be doubled during all such time of arrear and (a sign of the times) if it should happen that the work of the mines should be suspended by reason of war or the incursion of the nation's enemies (the Scots), a proportionate reduction was to be made from the rent. This appears to be the first recorded reference to coal-mining which was to dominate the life of Whickham for many hundreds of years. Towards the end of the century, Bishop Hatfield ordered another survey which was completed around 1382, almost exactly 200 years after the *Boldon Book*. The weakening of the old feudal structure is clearly evident, with the former villein/lord relationship being replaced by various forms of tenancies and the onerous labour commitments converted into money rents, but the overall picture is of a still predominantly agricultural community, which had successfully survived the troubles of the preceding century.

The Fifteenth and Sixteenth Centuries

The peaceful life suggested in the *Hatfield Survey* seems to have lasted for most of the next two hundred years with the coal-mining industry gradually developing, albeit still on a very small scale, and the landed gentry flourishing in consequence. This progress was rudely interrupted in 1569 when the Earls of Northumberland and Westmorland led a rebellion intended to re-establish the Roman Catholic religion in England. Initially, the earls gathered about 2,000 friends and supporters but this number more than doubled as they moved south through Durham, apparently en route to Tutbury in Staffordshire to release Mary, Queen of Scots, from her place of internment. Ahead of them, however, were the Earls of Essex and Warwick with very much larger forces, and behind them Sir George Bowes, an ancestor of the Bowes of Gibside, was raising another army in the bishopric. After a minor victory at Barnard Castle, the rebel earls realized that they faced inevitable defeat and retreated, first to Hexham and then to Naworth Castle and into the safety of Liddesdale and Teviotdale. Severe punishment was levied on those who had supported the rebellion. Sixty-six were executed in Durham City, and Sir George Bowes boasted that in an area of the county 60 miles by 20 miles there was hardly a town or village where he had not executed at least one of the inhabitants. In Whickham, two of the rebels were publicly executed, probably on the village green. The last years of the century saw more than one visitation of 'pestilence', or the plague, and food was at famine prices – an opportunity for profit which some were quick to seize. In 1587, the *Annals of Whickham* record that 'manye poore people

Dockendale Hall as it was in 1944.

weare supposed to die for lacke of bredde, not withstandyng greatte store in the handes of hard harted carles, yt styll raysed the p'ce [price] untyll harvest; at wyche tyme ye p'ce of corn begane to fall'.

The Seventeenth Century

The seventeenth century began with several hard winters, more outbreaks of the plague and the first of a series of entries in the parish records concerning men who had been 'slayne in a pitt' – a reflection of the dangers inherent in the developing coal-mining industry. In 1640, the English were defeated by the Scots at the Battle of Stella Haughs (or Newburn) on the Tyne a short distance from Whickham. After their defeat, they rested in the fields behind Whickham parish church but the Scots pursued them up the bank and, having insufficient time to dismantle their encampment, the English set fire to their tents. This fire set fire to an outcrop of coal, which burned for several years leaving a stratum of burned stones and earth which was still visible until quite recently.

This defeat by the Scots caused panic among the people of Whickham, and a pamphlet written about the battle at the time records that 'The parsons of Rye (*Ryton*), and of Whickham, first

rifled their own houses and fled, leaving nothing but a few play books and pamphlets, and one old cloak, with an old woman, being the only living christian in the towne; the rest being fled.' In 1650, the English obtained their revenge when Oliver Cromwell defeated the Scots at the Battle of Dunbar. En route to Scotland, the majority of the English army went through Newcastle, but the artillery passed through Whickham, down Clockburn Lane to ford the Derwent at its foot and then through the Axwell Park estate (held by the Royalist Clavering family) to ford the Tyne at Newburn. At this time Cromwell is believed to have stayed at Dockendale Hall in Whickham, also held by a Royalist family. An event of considerable importance took place towards the end of the century when Crowley's Iron Works were established in the area in 1691, initially at Winlaton Mill and subsequently in Swalwell where they played a considerable role in the development of the community.

The Eighteenth and Nineteenth Centuries

Towards the end of the eighteenth century, the impact of mining had produced a village in which the attractiveness of the central parts was offset by the depressing appearance of the surrounding area. William Hutchinson, a local historian, summed this up in 1787 when he wrote that 'The town of Whickham hangs on the brow of a hill with an open eastern aspect; the chief buildings, which are many of them modern and handsome, stand on the south side, on the brink of a steep descent, so as to overlook the rest of the town. The prospect is remarkably beautiful, comprehending part of Gateshead, with the church, the tower of St Nicholas in Newcastle, the castle, and much of the town on the margin of the river; to the right, Gateshead Fell, patched with innumerable cottages, quarries, wind mills, and other objects; to the left, the pleasant villages of Ryton, Benwell, Elswick, Newburn, Leamington.' This euphoric picture of the village is then offset by Hutchinson's description of the adjacent country which 'wears an unpleasant aspect to the traveller, cut and harrowed up with loaded carriages, scattered over with mean cottages, from whence swarm forth innumerable inhabitants, maintained by working in the mines; where many a sooty face is seen by every hedge-way side. The workmen earn great wages, which recompense every other evil. The meagreness of the track by which you pass to the environs of Gibside, renders the scene more striking.'

During the eighteenth and nineteenth centuries, although Whickham itself remained a peaceful community, its industries benefited from the wars in which the country was involved, notably the war with revolutionary and post-revolutionary France. In 1803, for example, when a French invasion was feared, Crowley's Iron Works produced a chain to be placed across the River Tyne to prevent the passage of French ships up-river during the hours of darkness. Around the same time, a parish meeting led to the creation of a 500 strong Corps of Volunteers under the command of Lord Strathmore with a view to defending the area against the French. Although the attack by the French never materialized, the Volunteers were well rewarded. Lord Strathmore presented the privates with a fat ox and a number of sheep, his wife entertained the officers at Gibside and Lady Liddell presented them with colours. Sadly, the disappearance of the perceived threat from the French after the Battle of Waterloo led to a depression in the iron trade; soup kitchens had to be set up and many skilled workers were employed to perform unskilled manual work on the roads at poverty rates of pay. Epidemics of smallpox and cholera followed in 1823 and 1831. Despite these setbacks, Whickham continued to develop and in 1834 was described as a 'large and respectable village' with clean and comfortable cottages, six farms, three public gardens, five inns, two doctors and several shops. By 1857 these had been joined by a fourth public garden, a reading room, a library and a post office. During the second half of the nineteenth century, the growth in population was such that the parish was divided into four, new churches being built in Dunston, Marley Hill and Swalwell.

Twentieth Century
In common with the rest of the country, the first half of the twentieth century was overshadowed by the loss of life in two world wars, the names of the fallen being recorded on the war memorials erected in each of the four parishes which now made up Whickham.

The second half of the century, in contrast, saw an enormous growth in population as Whickham developed as a suburb of the Tyneside conurbation. The massive housing development seems temporarily to have stopped but much of the open countryside which formerly surrounded the village is now covered with houses. Corresponding developments in the centre of the village have involved the demolition of some old housing to make way for improved shopping facilities. Outside pressures have generated a number of other major changes in the area.

The A1 (Gateshead Western Bypass) between Swalwell and Dunston. The Metro Centre is on the left.

In the late 1930s, the need to attract industry to the Tyneside area led to the development of the Team Valley Trading Estate to the east of Whickham. This was opened by King George VI in 1939, but nowadays, reflecting our changing economy, houses more offices than heavy industry.

In the 1970s, a new Western Bypass (now part of the A1) was built through Dunston and Swalwell to divert traffic away from central Tyneside. Around the same time, a national reorganization of local government led to Whickham being absorbed into a new Gateshead Metropolitan Borough.

In the 1980s, the Gateshead Metro Centre was developed in the area between Swalwell and Dunston, adjoining the new bypass, and the Northern Clubs Federation Brewery moved from Newcastle, where it suffered from a restricted site, into Dunston on a site near the Metro Centre. In the sporting field, Swalwell Cricket Club celebrated its centenary in 1980 and in the following year, Whickham AFC won the FA Vase at Wembley.

In 1990, Gateshead was responsible for a highly successful National Garden Festival on a number of sites centred around the lower reaches of the Team River. In addition to providing local people (and many visitors from other parts of the country) with a most enjoyable series of summer experiences, this resulted in the reclamation of many semi-derelict areas including the former Norwood Coke-Works and the area around the Dunston Staiths.

Throughout the decade, Whickham continued to win awards every year in the Britain in Bloom competitions, competing in the Large Town category although residents continue to refer to Whickham as 'the village'.

CHAPTER 2

Coal-mining and Wagonways

As will be apparent from the previous chapter, throughout its early history Whickham was essentially a rural community engaged in agricultural pursuits. Nevertheless, coal had been used as a fuel since Roman times, collected from the surface wherever it outcropped and used on domestic fires. However, coal had no particular advantages over wood, which was freely available at the time, and in consequence the use of coal for domestic heating remained a very small-scale activity.

By the fourteenth century, there were increasing demands for coal to be used for lime-burning and in smithies, and the scale of operations began to increase, slowly at first, and then more rapidly with the early stages of the Industrial Revolution. Tyneside had an important advantage in this growing market. In the days before the development of the railways and canals, when roads were both poorly built and maintained, coal could be easily shipped down the Tyne and round the coast to London and the South East.

In Whickham, seams tilted away from the river, so that coal outcropped on the slope down to the Tyne on the north side of the village, but became progressively deeper as one moved away from the river in a southerly direction. Initially, therefore, short tunnels or drifts were driven into the bank-side to get at the more readily accessible coal which was then transported downhill to the river in horses and carts (or wains).As the more accessible coal was exhausted, mining had to move further away from the river, shallow shafts were then sunk to the level of the seam and worked sideways into the coal as far as was safe when another shaft was sunk a short distance away. A windlass or 'jack roll' was used to lower men to the working level and to raise coal to the surface in wicker baskets or 'corves' holding about 4 ½ cwts. This type of pit was known as a bell-pit because of the shape of the excavation which resulted. As each shaft entailed a certain amount of initial unproductive work in digging down to the level of the seam before coal could be extracted (perhaps 30ft or more in even the shallowest pits), there was always a temptation to get the maximum value out of each pit by working an extra foot or two away from the shaft before facing the job of sinking a new shaft. In the circumstances it is

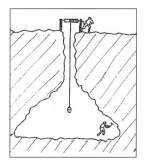

Sketch of a bell-pit.

not perhaps surprising that the parish records of the time contain many references to men being 'slayne in a pit' – generally because they had been buried when a bell-pit collapsed. Traces of these early mine-workings are still visible in the 'banky fields' between Whickham and Dunston.

As mining activities were forced to move further and further away from the river in search of fresh reserves, shafts became ever deeper creating a range of problems which led, for example, to the development of winding gear to replace ladders, pumps to deal with the problem of drainage, fans to move air round the workings, improved and safer lighting, better roof supports and so on. More extensive workings were needed to make the deep shafts economically viable, so underground transport systems became necessary, and on the surface the distance of the new collieries from the river made it essential to find a replacement for the horse and cart.

Coal-mining in Whickham

The lease of all the mines in Whickham and Gateshead by Bishop Bury in 1356 has already been mentioned. From this time on, several thousand tons of coal were mined each year throughout the fourteenth and fifteenth centuries. The combined manors of Whickham were among the very few places where coal was transported more than a few miles from its source and earned more than a few pounds per annum.

Although the 1356 lease was the first record of coal-mining in the parish records many other references followed. In 1402, for example, John de Hall was 'brought before the Court for not

A medieval drawing showing the complexities of deep mining before the development of winding gear to replace ladders.

carrying coals from the coalpit to the Derwent whereby John de Tynedale suffered damage to the amount of 13s.' Presumably the damages resulted from business being lost. Some years later 'it is found by the jury that John de Penrith is injured by a coalmine of Roger de Thornton, so that the house of the said John is almost thrown down, to the damage of the said of 20s, assessed by the jury; therefore, it is considered that the said Roger repair the said house to the value aforesaid, or satisfy the said sum.' Other Bishops also had dealings in the mines. In 1529, for example, Cardinal Wolsey, who was Bishop of Durham at the time, appointed 'William Thomlyngson, keeper of Gateshead Park, and his son William, to the office of clerk to all his mines, as well as that of lead and iron, as of coals, within his said desmesne lands of Durham, to receive daily one chaldron of coals out of each coalmine within the desmesnes of Gateshead, Whickham and Lynn Dean.' (In Tyneside, a chaldron was 53cwts.).In 1548, Bishop Tunstall leased one mine in Whickham to John and Stephen Sotheran for twenty-one years at a rent of £20 per annum. The Sotherans subsequently bought out the Thomlyngsons' remaining interest and in 1550, the Bishop devised to them the remaining collieries in Whickham and Gateshead subject to a payment of £10 for each new pit opened. In 1570, Bishop Pilkington leased to a group of Newcastle merchants the coalmining within an area bounded by 'the Whaggs and Newfield on the north, Gellesfield on the south, the Cross Moor on the west and the road to Newcastle and the Street Gate on the east' with a proviso that only three pits were to be opened at the same time. The increasing sophistication of the business is reflected in a lease of mines in the South Field five years later which included provision for a wayleave to a staith on the river.

Later in the century, in 1582, a lease known as the 'Grand Lease' was negotiated with Thomas Sutton under which Bishop Barnes gave up all control over coal-mining in the manor of Whickham for ninety-nine years in return for a rent of £117 15s 8d. Sutton's astute business dealings are reflected in the fact that he was able to sell his rights a year later for £12,000. The area went on to produce over 100,000 tons of coal per annum during the seventeenth century – more than any area of equal size anywhere in the world. New lease negotiations in the late seventeenth and early eighteenth centuries resulted in William Cotesworth, who became lord of the manor of both Whickham and Gateshead, obtaining a lease for his son-in-law, Alderman William Ramsay of Newcastle.

By the early eighteenth century, most of the more accessible and better quality seams in Whickham had been exhausted and although the production of low-quality coal continued until well after the Second World War, the great days of coal-mining in the area were over. In total, however, coal-mining played a major part in the life of Whickham for over 600 years.

The last colliery in Whickham village was Axwell Park Colliery which opened in 1839 and closed in 1953. There was only a man-riding shaft in Whickham which stood near the top of Whickham Bank, and coal was actually brought to the surface in Swalwell. In 1900 a dinner was held underground to raise money for the parish church.

Wagonways

As has already been mentioned, the North East coalfields' great advantage in the early days of coal-mining was in the availability of water to transport coal round the coast to London and the South East. The early pits were close to the Tyne and coal was transported down the river-banks and loaded into keels, boats with a shallow draught, which transported the coal down-river for trans-shipment into sea-going vessels.

As the shallower seams close to the river were worked out, pits were moved further and further away from the river which created an ever-worsening problem of getting coal from the pit to the river.

Axwell Pit Head,
Whickham, c. 1920.

Initially wains, that is horse-drawn carts, continued to be used for this purpose, and it has been estimated that in the late seventeenth and early eighteenth centuries at least 700 wains were in daily use for the transport of coal in the Whickham area. The disastrous effects of this horse-drawn traffic on the fields, paths and roadways of the district may easily be imagined, particularly in winter when the roads became virtually impassable. In addition, the coal-owners had to obtain wayleaves from the landowners between pit and river, that is permission to transport coal over their lands, and the rents for these were often exorbitant. At the same time, the farm land often suffered greatly, which was well illustrated in a court case of 1633. In 1620, Thomas Liddell of Ravensworth, who was a former Mayor of Newcastle and whose descendants were to become Lords Ravensworth, obtained a wayleave from local copyholders allowing wains to carry coal over their land from his pits to staiths on the River Team. This agreement was apparently satisfactory to all parties until 1633 when the copyholders 'did take and uniustlie detayne' six wains together with twelve oxen and twelve horses which were pulling them. When Liddell sued them, the copyholders adopted a two-pronged defence – either (i) the agreement did not exist at all, or (ii) if it did exist, it related to only two pits and was restricted to seven yards wide, for which a rent of £10 was payable plus 2s per wain. Now, the copyholders complained, there were many more pits involved, some of them not belonging to Liddell, and he 'hathe beaten out the same wayes by his said carryages in some places to Twenty fower yeardes or thereaboutes and that by reason thereof such great quantityes of dust be raised that the pasture arrable adioyninge to those wayes are much spoiled.' One can see their point. The judgement split the difference and specified a maximum width of sixteen yards wide for the route which Liddell could continue using provided he made 'watergates, trenches and ditches' to remove surface water and paid extra if non-Ravensworth pits were involved. What was clearly needed was some more efficient and economical means of transport which carried more coal, more quickly, with fewer horses (or oxen) and without interruption caused by winter weather conditions. The answer which eventually emerged was the wagonway, a forerunner of the modern railway.

Wagonways were railways in the sense that they consisted of rails laid along a prepared surface so that vehicles running along them could not, under normal circumstances, leave the track. They

The heading of an Allerton Colliery map in 1786 showing a horse gin, Newcomen engine, keel and horse-drawn wagonway.

differed from modern railways in that the rails were made from wood rather than iron or steel, and the vehicles were moved along them by hand, by means of horses or, where the terrain allowed it, by gravity rather than steam, diesel or electricity.

As experience was gained in the construction of these ways, the track was designed so that gravity was the main motive power taking the loaded wagons from pit to river and horses pulled the empties back to the pit. This entailed looking for roughly easy gradients in the right direction and then dealing with 'humps and

A horse-drawn wagonway from the heading of a map of Tyneside by John Gibson in 1787. It has been suggested that this may be a (slightly romanticized) drawing of Gateshead. Remarkably, the mysterious object to the left of the colliery even looks like the modern Angel of the North and is in roughly the right situation.

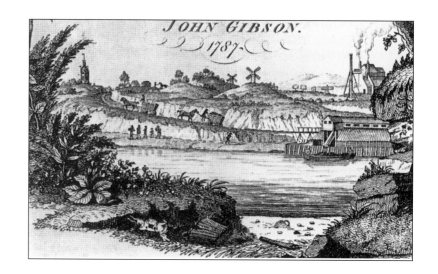

hollows' by constructing cuttings, embankments and even bridges where necessary.

Wayleaves continued to be a problem although, as a last resort, coal-owners could petition the Privy Council for a compulsory wayleave, requests which were often granted on grounds of the 'common good'. The 'Grand Lease', which William Cotesworth had obtained for his son-in-law, Alderman Ramsay, reverted to Cotesworth when Ramsay died in 1716. Cotesworth become lord of the manor in the same year and acquired control over wayleaves in the area which he proceeded to exploit in a ruthless manner.

In 1726, a group of coal-owners, comprising George Bowes of Gibside, the Liddells of Ravensworth, and the Montagues and Thomas Ord of Newcastle, formed a partnership popularly known as the 'Grand Allies' to buy out Cotesworth, thereby acquiring control of both the collieries and the wayleaves in the most profitable coal-mining area in England.

The Tanfield Railway

The Tanfield Railway, running between Dunston and Tanfield, began life as one of the first wagonways ever built. The actual date of its initial construction is unknown, although there was clearly a wagonway in the general area in the mid-seventeenth century, because entries in Whickham parish records refer to people being 'slaine near the waggon way' or 'slaine by a waggon' in the Dunston area as early as 1650. The Grand Allies acquired it as part of their 1726 purchase and proceeded to improve the gradients by means of cuttings and embankments so that movement to the staiths was assisted by gravity and the horse-power needed was minimized. These developments included the construction of a single arch stone bridge over the Causey Burn known as the Causey Arch. This was completed in 1727, making it the oldest stone railway bridge in the world and, as such, it is listed as an ancient monument. Paradoxically, a serious fire at the colliery which the bridge had been built to serve led to its being taken out of use in 1740 and the line re-routed so the Tanfield's most famous feature had a very short working life.

The Allies also built a massive embankment over the valley of the Beckley Burn which is 300 feet wide at the base and 100 feet high and is believed to be the oldest railway embankment in the world still in use. This, although perhaps less striking to look at, is in some ways an even more notable achievement than the Causey Arch when one remembers that it was constructed entirely with

The Causey Arch, 1804.

pick and shovel. Indeed, it has been properly pointed out that nothing on this scale had been built since Roman times and people came from far and wide to look at it.

At its maximum extent, the Tanfield ran from Dunston to Beamish, Shield Row and South Moor – a distance of eight miles – making it, for a time, the longest wagonway on Tyneside. With the development of steam power, the line was organized to use the most efficient form of traction on each section: self-acting inclines (where the descending full wagons were used to haul up empty wagons by means of a connecting cable) on the steepest sections, stationary steam engines on shallower slopes and horses on the relatively flat sections.

The Tanfield was rebuilt as a predominantly loco-hauled line in 1839 but even then still made use of self-acting inclines and stationary steam engines to deal with gradients.

The line finally closed only in 1964 having been in active use for over 300 years. Part of it is now operated by a steam preservation society and most of the route is still traceable as a country footpath.

Other Wagonways

Despite the long life and resulting fame of the Tanfield Railway, it was only one of a number of wagonways which were built in the Whickham area. Among other very early Whickham lines were the Whickham Grand Lease, Team, Riding Field, Dunston (or Northbanks), Bucks Nook, and Old and New Western Ways. Unlike the Tanfield, most of these had fairly short lives, being built in the seventeenth century and closed less than a hundred years later, although in one or two cases sections of the original route stayed in use as steam railways well into the twentieth century. The map illustrates the remarkable extent of the wagonway network in and around Whickham about the beginning of the eighteenth century.

Part of the reason for the proliferation of lines was the personal animosities which existed between the various coal-

The point at Marley Hill Colliery where the Tanfield line crossed the Bowes Railway on the level.

A map showing the wagonways in Whickham at their greatest extent in the late seventeenth and early eighteenth centuries.

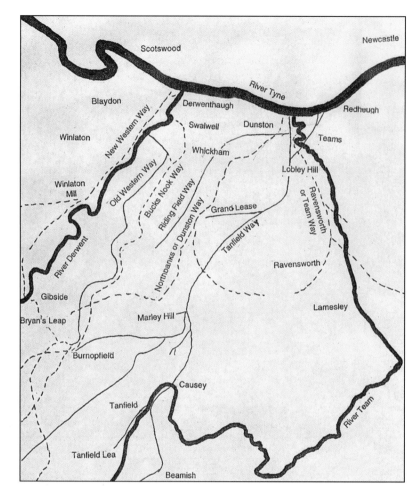

A loaded set with man-rider about to descend the Lobley Hill incline on the Tanfield railway.

owners. The Bucks Nook line was built because Sir John Clavering and Thomas Brumell were not on good terms with the Bowes and Montagues who controlled the Dunston Way. The legal right to use part of the route was in dispute which led to a hostile crowd, led by Lady Bowes in person and supported by William Cotesworth, tearing up part of the track before it was finally opened in 1712. William Bowes, Lady Bowes' son, subsequently built the Western Way which was parallel to, and sometimes only yards away from, the Bucks Nook with which it was intended to compete.

In the meantime, pits were being progressively worked out, and in 1739, a new Western Way was built down Busty Bank and along the western bank of the River Derwent to serve collieries further south. This resulted in the final demise of the remaining competing lines in Whickham with the exception of the Tanfield. Remarkably, traces of some of these very early

The remains of an embankment on the Dunston wagonway adjoining Washingwell Lane. The line closed in 1725.

An embankment on the Old Western wagonway running parallel to Fellside Road. The line closed in 1738.

lines still exist. Embankments and cuttings of the Dunston Way still exist either side of Whickham Highway as it enters Whickham and are mentioned in the Walking Tour section of this book. Another embankment and a cutting associated with either the Old Western Way or the Bucks Nook, it is not clear which, are visible in fields to the west of Fellside Road near the East Byermoor Guest House.

CHAPTER 3

The Landed Gentry

As might be expected from the dominance of coal-mining in the local economy for so many years, the wealth of the local landed gentry was derived not so much from the land itself as from the mineral resources which lay beneath it, and the rise and fall of the great estates tended to follow the rise and decline of the mining industry.

The Liddells of Ravensworth

Ravensworth was first mentioned about 1070 and the estate was held over the centuries by many famous families including the Fitzwilliams and the Gascoignes from whom the Liddells acquired it in 1607. The Liddells were a local business family who made most of their money out of mining. The family provided several Sheriffs and Lord Mayors of Newcastle as well as a number of MPs, eventually acquiring the title of Lord Ravensworth in 1747, but the best known member of the family was probably Alice Liddell who became the model for the Alice of *Alice in Wonderland*.

Ravensworth Castle, ancestral home of the Liddell family, c. 1910.

Ravensworth Castle was extensively re-modelled and enlarged around the beginning of the nineteenth century to the design of the John Nash who also designed Regent Street in London and the Brighton Pavilion. At the beginning of the twentieth century, death duties on three successive deaths in sixteen years caused the financial downfall of the family, and the castle and its contents were sold in 1920. The building was used as a school for a time and then started to crumble, ironically because of the mineworkings below, so the coal on which the family fortune was based also undermined it. The estate was largely destroyed by opencast working, intensive farming and the mass felling of trees, and was finally sold off, mainly to tenants, in 1976.

The Hardings of Hollinside
Hollinside Manor House is the second oldest surviving building in Whickham after the church and like the church is a Grade I listed building. It is in ruins, but Tyne and Wear County Council, which carried out an enormous amount of conservation work before its abolition by the Government, put a good deal of effort into preserving what is left.

The building appears to date from the thirteenth century, and the thickness of the walls suggest that it served a similar purpose to a pele tower, being designed for defensive purposes rather than comfort at a time when the Scots and moss-troopers posed a constant threat.

The ruins of Hollinside Manor, former home of the Harding family, subsequently part of the Gibside estate.

The earliest reference to the Hollinside estate was in 1317 when it was in the possession of Thomas de Hollinside and included a water mill and fishery on the Derwent. It changed hands several times over the following century, passing through the hands of the de Boines, Burtons or Burdons, Massams and Redheughs before finally being acquired by the Hardings through the marriage in 1430 of Roger Harding to a daughter of the Redheughs. Roger Harding was a descendant of Sampson Harding who had been Mayor of Newcastle from 1396 to 1399 and MP for the city. The Hardings were apparently very large people, legend suggesting that they were over 7ft tall in some cases, and they became known as the 'Giants of Hollinside', Hollinside itself being known as the 'Giants' Castle' and a nearby quarry as the 'Giants' Quarry'. They originated from Beadnell in Northumberland, where one of the family served as a page to Sir Henry Percy (Hotspur), fought at the Battle of Homildon Hill and was subsequently Warden of Warkworth Castle under Henry IV. In 1730, the family's mines and staiths at Derwenthaugh failed, and the estate passed into the hands of George Bowes of Gibside and became part of the Gibside estate. The Hardings, however, remained in the neighbourhood of Gibside, because for several years after they lost possession of Hollinside, the Gibside estate records show payments to them for supplying corn, grass, hay and coal and for shooting crows, magpies and buzzards.

The Bowes of Gibside

Gibside is, of course, the best-known local estate and can be traced back to 1200 when it was held by the Marleys of Marley Hill. It subsequently passed into the hands of another well-known local family, the Blakistons or Blaxtons, in 1540, and then, through the marriage of Elizabeth Blakiston to Sir William Bowes, to the Bowes family in 1694. Gibside Hall was actually built by the Blakistons in 1620, but the man who created the lawns, lakes, gardens, avenues and terraces was George Bowes in the mid-eighteenth century. He was very interested in horse-racing and created a mile-long avenue of trees along which races were held. At one end of the avenue is the Chapel, designed by James Paine, which was started in 1760 but was not finished until 1812, long after George Bowes had died. At the other end is the Column of British Liberty, 140ft tall and surmounted by a statue 12ft high holding a staff carrying a Phrygian cap of liberty. Both the Chapel and the Column are Grade I listed buildings.

*Gibside Hall, now a
Grade II listed building,
originally built by
the Blakiston family
between 1603 and
1620, but later acquired
by Sir William Bowes
through marriage.*

There are many other historically important buildings on the Gibside estate including the Banqueting House, which is another Grade I listed building, and the hall itself, the orangery, stables, ice house, Chapel House, sundial, piers and walls which are all Grade II. One of the most interesting events in the history of the Bowes family was the marriage of Mary Eleanor Bowes, the daughter of George Bowes and a very wealthy heiress, to John Lyon, Earl of Strathmore of Glamis Castle, in 1767. This marriage gave rise to the Bowes-Lyon family from which Elizabeth, the Queen Mother is descended. Sadly, the Earl died nine years later and Mary Eleanor married an adventurer called Stoney who became known as Stoney Bowes.

*Gibside Chapel, a
Grade I listed building,
was built by the Bowes
family between 1759
and 1812.*

Gibside Banqueting House, a Grade I listed building, was built 1738-1740.

This marriage was disastrous and is the subject of a well-known book, *The Unhappy Countess*. Stoney Bowes wasted much of his wife's estate, and treated her so harshly that she was forced to seek the protection of the courts. In 1787, he actually abducted her with a view to getting her to transfer the remainder of the estate to him and a melodramatic chase over the moors followed. He spent the rest of his life in prison still attempting to acquire control of his wife's wealth.

After a period during which Gibside was largely abandoned apart from the chapel, the estate has now been acquired by the National Trust which has put its resources into preserving the buildings, restoring the grounds and opening them up to the public.

Many of the estate records still survive and make fascinating reading today. Most of the entries relate, as might be expected, to the running of the Gibside estate, but in 1739 there are a number of entries relating to George Bowes' election expenses which included quite substantial sums 'expended this month amongst freeholders as per particulars in ye file' and 'laid out in drink, ...on treating freeholders'. There are also items reflecting purely domestic matters. In 1771, for example, the Whickham bell-ringers were paid for ringing the church bells on Lord Strathmore's birthday and another payment was made for 'making six pairs of red shoes for Lady Maria'. Perhaps the oddest entry in that year, however, refers to the purchase of 'two pairs of stays for Lord Glamis'.

Axwell Hall, on the west side of the Derwent, was built by Sir Thomas Clavering in 1760 to replace the Claverings' previous home in Old Axwell, Whickham.

The Claverings of Axwell Park

Axwell was another very old estate in Whickham which was first mentioned in 1318 in connection with the purchase of Hollinside Manor by William de Boine. Like Hollinside, it passed through many hands over the years including William de Birtley, the Redheughs, Thorntons, Lumleys, Ogles and Selbys and was eventually acquired by another well-known local family, the Claverings, in 1629. At this time the estate was based at what was known as 'Old Axwell', but this house no longer exists and the estate has been absorbed into the Fellside Park housing estate. In 1760, the Claverings built the present Axwell Park on the other side of the River Derwent to designs by James Paine. The family played a considerable part in the affairs of the North of England, providing a High Sheriff of County Durham and a Sheriff and

The lake in Axwell Park estate.

Mayor of Newcastle. Sir Thomas Clavering, who represented County Durham in four parliaments in the eighteenth century was supported in his first campaign by John Wesley. The last Clavering died in 1893, and the hall passed into the hands of another branch of the family before being sold and turned into a boys' school at the end of the First World War.

The Clavering family were of Norman origin and other branches of the family held land in many parts of the country. One branch became Barons of Warkworth with claims to the throne of Scotland, and three branches of the family were represented among the barons who forced King John to sign the Magna Carta.

The Carrs of Dunston Hill

Dunston Hill estate originally belonged to the Shaftoe family of 'Bobby Shaftoe' fame but was purchased by John Carr in 1704, and it was his son Ralph whose business success enabled him to enlarge the estate and build the present hall around 1760. Ralph's eldest son, another John, married Hannah Ellison and it was their son, another Ralph, who added the name Ellison to his own to become Ralph Carr-Ellison in 1870. Ralph Carr-Ellison was an accomplished man who, in addition to being a Greek and Latin scholar, could speak many European languages. He was also interested in antiquarian studies and read numerous papers before the Newcastle Society of Antiquaries. He also served for a time as High Sheriff of Northumberland. In Whickham he was a well-known local benefactor, popularly known as 'the Squire'.

Ralph Carr-Ellison's younger brother was the Revd Henry Byne Carr, Rector of Whickham for fifty years from 1846 to

Dunston Hill, ancestral home of the Carr (later Carr-Ellison) family.

1896, who made an immense contribution to the affairs of the village. A well educated man, like his brother, his early education began at the boarding school which existed at that time in Beech House, Whickham, where his brothers Ralph and Charles were fellow pupils along with William, later Lord, Armstrong. From there he went on to Ripon Grammar school, then to University College, Oxford, where he took his MA, and finally to Durham University for theological training. He was ordained in 1836 and was appointed to Whickham in 1846 after service as a curate elsewhere. Although a strong adherent of the Church of England he was also a great admirer of John Wesley and was a generous benefactor of the Methodist Sunday school when it was set up in Whickham.

In 1852, following the attempt by a man called Atkins to turn the village green into a quarry (described in Chapter 7), the Revd Carr purchased the house in which Atkins lived and persuaded his brother to purchase the green and present it to the people of Whickham. The brothers were also prime movers in the rebuilding of the church following the disastrous fire earlier in the century, and the Revd Carr was responsible for churches in Dunston in 1873, at Marley Hill in 1877 and at Swalwell in 1894. Dunston Hill house and grounds were offered to the Whickham Urban District Council in 1914, and it was proposed to turn the grounds into a public park, but with the outbreak of the First World War, the estate was leased to the War Office for use as a temporary hospital, and it has remained a hospital ever since although now owned by the Health Authority.

The present Sir Ralph Carr-Ellison lives in Northumberland but has continued the family tradition of public service over many years. In Whickham, he is currently Patron of the Friends of the Parish Church of St Mary the Virgin, reflecting his family's long association with the church.

CHAPTER 4

Swalwell

Swalwell is situated near the mouth of the Derwent at the foot of
the hill leading up to Whickham and, although historically a
separate community with its own strong traditions, is now effectively
joined to Whickham to form one continuous, predominantly
residential area.

There is no generally accepted explanation of where the name
Swalwell came from although there is no shortage of suggestions.
In some of the earliest records, the name had an 's' on the end
– Swalwells – and the 'wells' part of the name clearly reflects the
fact that Swalwell used to be full of wells. William Bourn, in his
History of Whickham Parish mentions Roger's Well to the east of
the village, Hodgson's Well to the west, and the Spout in the

*A map of Swalwell as it
was in 1898.*

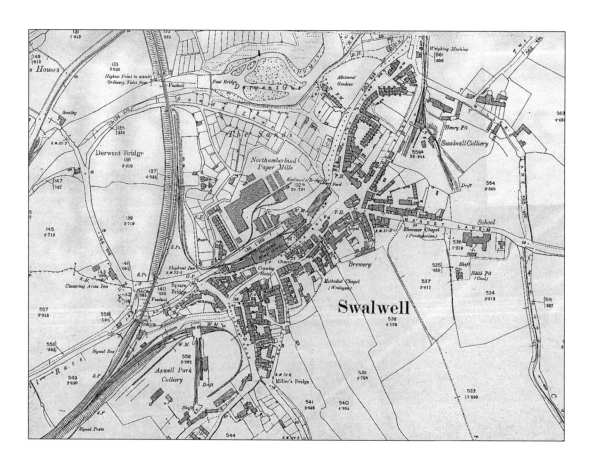

SWALWELL, WEST END.

middle. Other sources mention the Coaly Well in Coalway Lane midway between Swalwell and Whickham, the Tea Well not far from Swalwell Station, the Coffee Well near the Parish church, and the Spa Well around a mile to the west, the water from which was supposed to cure many ills. Some of these may duplicate each other under different names but even so there were clearly very many wells in the area. However, it is the first part of the name which presents the problem.

The suggestions which are most frequently advanced link the prefix 'Swal' with the word swallow referring either to the bird (presumably because of large numbers of these birds in the area in the past) or to the process of swallowing the water. A much more likely explanation, in the author's opinion, is that the name is linked with the old word 'swale' meaning valley, and that 'Swalwells' meant 'the wells in the valley' which would have been a very accurate description of Swalwell in the past. Like Whickham, Swalwell was not covered by the *Domesday Book*, because it was part of Durham which was a County Palatine where the King's authority was replaced by that of the all-powerful Bishop of Durham. However, again like Whickham, Swalwell appears in the *Boldon Book*, prepared for Bishop Pudsey in 1183, which records that:

The west end of Swalwell, c. 1900. The branch railway line ran to the steel-works and paper-mill. The white houses at the right were at the foot of Swalwell Bank which led up to Whickham through fields now covered with houses. The large building in the centre was the Elephant Inn.

Swalwell Town Gate, c. 1900, showing the birth-place of William Shield in the centre. Only the Three Tuns now remains.

> *The land of Swalwell renders 16s. William, son of Arnald, for a clearing of 120 acres, renders one mark.*

There is no reference to a community at all, which suggests that whoever occupied 'the land of Swalwell' and William may have lived elsewhere, perhaps in Whickham itself. By the time of the *Hatfield Survey* 200 years later, a community seems to have developed because the survey records that:

> *The tenants jointly hold the mill of Swalwell [this was a water mill rather than a windmill], the fishery there, and the toll of ale, and used to pay £38, now only £20.*

At the beginning of the fifteenth century, Swalwell appears to have belonged to William de Swalwells, who was a burgess of Newcastle, but the estate subsequently passed through the hands of several different families, including the Lumleys, until finally, in 1629 it passed into the hands of the Claverings, in whose hands it remained until fairly recent times.

Crowley's Ironworks

Throughout most of its history, Swalwell probably consisted of too few houses to be even classed as a village. This all changed with the arrival of Sir Ambrose Crowley at the end of the seventeenth century.

Crowley opened his first works in the Winlaton area in 1690, and then extended these, first to Winlaton Mill a short distance up the Derwent, and then to Swalwell where they covered an area of four acres and comprised rolling mills, foundry, forges and smiths' shops. He advertised for men to make a variety of iron products ranging from anchors and chain cables to files, hammers, hinges and locks, but because there were few skilled workmen in the area he had to bring in many hundreds of workmen from the south of England and even from Spain and Germany, resulting in a massive increase in the population of the village. It is difficult to believe now, but in around 1770, Crowley's works were described as 'the greatest manufactory of its kind in Europe'.

Very little is known about the early life of this remarkable man except that he rose from humble beginnings as a smith to become the head of his own firm. He was knighted in 1706, was Sheriff of London in 1707, and died in 1713, at which time he was a London alderman and MP for Andover.

Crowley's main historical significance lies in the many very advanced ideas which he introduced into his business. For example, he introduced a code of laws for his employees, and a tribunal, known as 'Crowley's Court', which met every ten weeks and dealt not only with breaches of his code of laws but with disputes between employees, and social and financial wrongdoing. Shopkeepers and other tradespeople who were owed money could come to the Court, and if they proved their case, a fixed amount would be deducted from the employee's weekly wage until the debt had been paid off. Publicans, however, were not allowed to use the Court to recover amounts owing for drink.

Market Lane, Swalwell, looking west, 1909. The chimney is the sole surviving reminder of the steel-works.

Lady's Steps, c. 1900. The weir on the Derwent which diverted water into Crowley's mill-race was a favourite picnic spot.

Crowley also maintained 'personnel records' for all his employees covering not only their name and address, but also their age, religion, height, complexion and place of birth.

In addition, the firm employed a doctor to look after the workmen and operated both a company medical scheme and a pension scheme, the pensioners being required to wear armbands bearing the words 'Crowley's Poor'. The latter scheme was not free, however. A 'tax' of ninepence in the pound was levied on each employee's earnings, and used not only to finance the pension scheme but to provide accommodation, food and clothing for those who were sick or disabled. All these schemes were quite remarkable when it is remembered that they preceded the National Health Service by 250 years.

The Keelman's Bridge, c. 1910. This bridge across Crowley's mill-race led to allotments on the Sands, generally known as the Gardens. Both bridge and allotments have since disappeared under an access road to the A1.

The workers also contributed towards the employment of a chaplain (presumably by means of another 'tax') and set up a library in Winlaton. Crowley himself contributed towards the construction of a chapel in Winlaton, the provision of a large gallery for his workmen in Ryton church, and developed schools in both Winlaton Mill and Swalwell.

Despite Crowley's benevolence and forward thinking, however, his employees still had to work long hours by modern standards. In some departments, they worked from three in the morning until six at night. In others, they worked shifts commencing at midnight or three in the morning. Saturdays, however, were short days with some men working from three in the morning until one in the afternoon. The workmen who made the heavier goods were relatively well-paid but those who handled the lighter products were poorly paid, and labourers, who were mostly old men, received only 1s 6d a day.

The Crowley line ended in the late eighteenth century. The firm passed into the ownership of a Mr Millington and became known as Crowley Millington and Co. As ironworks developed elsewhere, the work gradually diminished at Swalwell until the factory was eventually closed. Despite the closure of Crowley's, Swalwell continued to function as an industrial centre. Two collieries and Swalwell Brewery provided employment and the existence of a skilled workforce attracted other iron works and various other manufacturing firms including, for example, R. and W. Shield, spade and shovel makers, and two brickworks.

Crowley's Crew

The workers at Crowley's, known as Crowley's Crew and usually led by 'Lang Jack' English whose story is told below, were famous for their Tory (Conservative) principles, while the keelmen in Swalwell were equally well known as supporters of the Whigs (modern Liberals). These differences often seem to have been little more than an excuse to indulge in general mischief-making. In 1793, for example, Crowley's men hanged and then burnt an effigy of Tom Paine, the great democrat, in Swalwell. On this occasion, even though a large number of people took part, everyone seems to have behaved very properly. Most people wore cockades and labels in their hats bearing patriotic slogans, and the proceedings ended with the National Anthem being sung and the firing of small arms and cannon. The following year, a much more violent confrontation took place between the two factions with a good deal of stone-throwing. The *Newcastle Advertiser* said that many of

Crowley's Crew 'narrowly escaped being murdered by a tumultuous assembly of keelmen and their wives'. Later on, Crowley's Crew are alleged to have issued a statement declaring their intention that 'should ever an attempt be made to disturb the Peace of the Factory, to unite as one Body in support of the present Government, and to defend the property of Messrs Crowley Millington and Co. as well as their own lives and families.'

As Crowley's faced increasing competition from other firms, and Swalwell's leadership in iron manufacturing gradually disappeared, the enthusiasm of Crowley's Crew for the Tory Government also diminished very considerably and they were among the first supporters of the Chartist movement in the North of England. In addition to holding private meetings in public houses to raise money and public meetings to listen to the views of leading Chartists, the workers used to drill at night-time in preparation for the anticipated troubles ahead. At times they acted as bodyguards to Charles Attwood of Whickham, who was a leading campaigner for the Reform movement in the early 1830s. In October 1831, Charles John Clavering of Axwell Park was due to preside at a demonstration in Durham, and it became known that a gang of men employed by the Marquis of Londonderry was going to be brought along to disrupt the meeting. Attwood organized a group of 300 of Crowley's Crew from Swalwell, Blaydon and Winlaton and armed them with oak staves. When the anticipated disruption began, Crowley's Crew rapidly disposed of the opposition and the meeting proceeded without further interruption.

Lang Jack

As indicated above, the usual leader and certainly the best-known member of Crowley's Crew, was John English, better known as Lang Jack, whose monument stands in the centre of Whickham.

Lang Jack was born around 1800, in Chester-le-Street, and moved to Whickham in 1830 to work on the Scotswood Suspension Bridge as a stonemason. He subsequently built the pillars for the old Butterfly Bridge across the River Derwent at the foot of Clockburn Lane and in 1848 worked on the renovation of Lamesley church. He was a very big man and it was his height of 6ft 4 ½ inches which gave rise to his nickname.

Jack subsequently moved to Whickham, and after living for a few years at the Wood House, Jack built his own house at the end of Woodhouse Lane, moving the stone himself from a nearby quarry by means of a bogey, and allegedly carrying the chimney tops (weighing about 1 ½ cwt each) on his shoulders from Blaydon

Lang Jack's cottage in Woodhouse Lane, c. 1900, with his monument still in situ. The cottage was built in 1830 and destroyed by fire in 1907.

Lang Jack's monument after re-erection in its new position in Whickham in 1976.

Bank quarry about four miles away. As this story indicates, Lang Jack was extremely strong and there are many tales about his feats of strength. On one occasion, for example, a cartman ran over and killed his dog, and Lang Jack was so enraged that he tipped the horse and cart, together with its load, over a nearby bank.

Eventually, Jack, who was always being tempted to perform feats to show off his great strength and also seems to have been a heavy drinker, over-taxed himself to the extent that he was unable to work in his later years and finally died in 1860 at the age of sixty. Before his death, however, an 18ft high column bearing his likeness in the form of a bust was erected opposite his cottage. It was designed and constructed by Mr John Norvell of Swalwell and bore the inscription 'J. English, 1854'. Lang Jack in consequence had the rare distinction of having a monument erected in his honour during his lifetime. A considerable crowd of people attended the unveiling and were subsequently led back to the village, where refreshments had been laid on, by Whickham Brass Band.

Jack's cottage remained in occupation until the beginning of the twentieth century when it caught fire and was destroyed. Lang Jack's monument, however, remained standing until 1976 when, 122 years after it was first erected, vandals finally toppled the bust from the top of its column and broke it into three pieces. At this time, Bellway, the building firm which now owned the land on which the column stood, came to the rescue, and as a goodwill gesture had the bust and column repaired and re-erected in the centre of Whickham where it still stands.

Swalwell Hoppings
The word 'hopping' seems to be derived from a Saxon word meaning to leap or dance, and in many places dances are still known as 'hops'. In the north east, however, 'hopping' means not just dancing but something much more like a carnival encompassing a whole range of sports and pastimes which eventually evolved into the great fair known as the Newcastle Hoppings which still takes place each year.

In the eighteenth and nineteenth centuries, Swalwell Hoppings were a great event in the local calendar and lasted a whole week. Among the major attractions were horse races on the area known as the Sands which attracted thousands of people from all over Tyneside, many of them arriving at Derwenthaugh, at the mouth of the Derwent, by steamboat. The open area in the centre of Swalwell known as the Town Gate housed the caravans and shows

which included Punch and Judy and exhibitions of wild animals.

In 1758, the diversions included 'dancing for ribands, grinning [now known as 'gurning'] for tobacco, women running for smocks, ass races, footcourses by men, with an odd whim of a man eating a cock alive, feathers, entrails and all'. If the last of these seems to be a very unpleasant piece of 'entertainment', it is worth remembering that bull-baiting, cock-fighting and other degrading activities were also popular at the time.

The main attractions of Swalwell Hoppings, however, were probably always dancing, eating, drinking and fighting. In 1828, Swalwell had a population of 1,320 served by thirteen public houses and its own brewery, so there was ample scope for drinking, and the drinking no doubt encouraged the fighting. As well as the traditional hostility between Crowley's Crew and the keelmen, feuds also existed between the workmen of Swalwell and Winlaton, and the hoppings were a suitable occasion to settle old scores. There were also 'dancings' held at every public house which were well attended by young people of both sexes. The Rector of Whickham so disapproved of this behaviour that on one occasion he rebuked the people of Swalwell from the pulpit of Whickham church. The next night a considerable number of Swalwell people marched to Whickham and attacked the Rectory, breaking all the windows with stones. This perhaps reflected another longstanding rivalry – between Swalwell and Whickham. By the end of the nineteenth century, Swalwell Hoppings had become a much quieter affair altogether, with stalls and fairground attractions, but without horse races and with none of the more outlandish pursuits of earlier times. Nowadays village hoppings seem to have disappeared altogether and the only survivor is the giant hoppings held on Newcastle Town Moor each year.

The Swalwell Cabbage

No account of Swalwell would be complete without reference to the Swalwell Cabbage. In the nineteenth century, Swalwell was renowned for the quality of its gardens and vegetable produce. The high spot of its horticultural history, however, probably occurred in 1865 when Mr W. Collingwood grew a red cabbage which stood 4ft 2in (127cm) high, measured 7yd 5in (653cm) round and weighed 8st 11lb (55.8Kg). This is claimed, with some justification, to be a world record and has passed into local folklore.

Swalwell Colliery, c. 1910. The colliery, which opened in 1839, finally closed in 1953.

Swalwell Station after its closure in 1962.

SANDS BRIDGE, SWALWELL

Swalwell Today

By the beginning of the twentieth century, Swalwell had lost much of its large scale industry. During the next 100 years, Swalwell changed even more dramatically. Council houses now fill what was formerly open country between Swalwell and Whickham. The Swalwell end of Axwell Park Colliery which had opened in 1839 finally closed in 1953. Swalwell Railway Station and the Derwent Valley branch line which had served the area since 1867 were closed to passenger traffic in 1953 and closed completely in 1962. The Western Bypass (now the A1) was driven through the area with the loss of a number of old houses, and the Metro Centre was built on what had been coal stocking ground.

The Swalwell of yesterday was an industrial township housing large scale industry. Today, despite the existence of a small number of industrial units, Swalwell is essentially a residential suburb of Tyneside.

The 'Hikey' foot-bridge over the River Derwent with the railway embankment and bridge (still in existence) in the background.

CHAPTER 5

Dunston

There is very little direct evidence available about the early history of Dunston because until quite recent times Dunston was treated merely as part of the parish of Whickham and it is rarely possible to identify items in the parish records which refer specifically to Dunston as against other parts of the parish. A reasonable assumption can, however, be made about one aspect of its early history – its fishing. Dunston is situated where the River Team joins the River Tyne and it was probably as a good source of salmon and other fish that it attracted its first settlers – possibly in prehistoric times. Certainly, when written records began to be kept from Norman times onwards, they contain many references to the value of the fisheries on the Tyne and these had no doubt existed long before the Normans arrived. It was in Norman times, however, following disputes about fishing rights, that the decision was originally made to divide the width of the river into three, the southern third to belong to the Bishop of Durham, the northern third to Northumberland and the middle third to be available

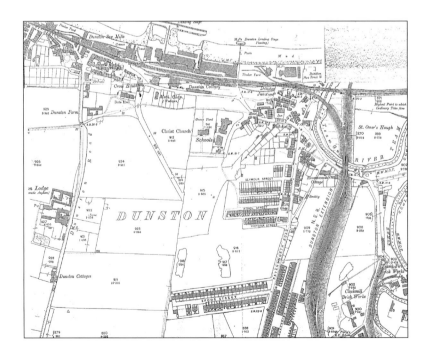

A map of Dunston as it was in 1898.

to both sides – a ruling which was of considerable importance in later years especially in relation to the control of the bridge (when there was only one) over the Tyne. The origin of the name Dunston is something of a puzzle although it can be traced back as far as 1328. 'Dun' usually means 'hill', and 'ton' means' town or settlement' (in Old English) so that Dunston can be interpreted as meaning 'hill-town'. This hardly describes today's Dunston which is mostly low and flat. It has been pointed out, however, that a large part of modern Dunston would have been under water or at least was marshy ground in the past, so that the earliest settlement is quite likely to have been in the area we now know as Dunston Hill, which makes the name Dunston seem much more sensible (and the name Dunston Hill less so as it would presumably mean 'hill-town hill'). In more recent times, Whickham was divided into four quarters and Dunston was known as Lowhand (the others were Whickham Township, Swalwell and Fellside) which suggest that the low-lying parts of Dunston had become more important than previously.

It is with the development of the coal-mining industry that Dunston begins to emerge from the mists of history because although, like Swalwell and unlike Whickham, Dunston developed as an industrial community, its roots were in the mining industry rather than engineering.

Dunston Colliery, with the CWS Soap Works and Flour Mills in the background, in the early years of the twentieth century. The colliery was opened in 1873 and closed in 1947.

Dunston had pits in 'Jack's Leazes' to the east of Dunston Bank (better known to locals as 'Carr's Bank' after the Carr family) and in the banky fields between Dunston and Whickham where evidence of mining activities can still be seen. There was also a pit in 'the parson's half-acre' in Dunston. As happened elsewhere, as coal reserves in the pits near the river became exhausted, mining activities were forced further and further inland. Beneath Dunston, however, the seams of coal were deep, narrow and faulted which made them difficult and expensive to work. In consequence, deep mining developed later in Dunston than elsewhere, the Norwood/ Farnacres Colliery (in the neighbourhood of St Philip Neri school) opening sometime prior to 1843 and closing in 1940, and the Dunston Colliery (on the site of Dunston Riverside school) opening in 1873 and closing in 1947.

Wagonways

What was much more significant in the history of Dunston, however, was the development of the wagonway system discussed earlier. In addition to its access to the River Team, Dunston was one of the few places on Tyneside (Swalwell/Derwenthaugh was another) with a sufficient area of flat land on which to provide storage facilities for large quantities of coal. In consequence, Dunston played a pioneering role in the development of wagonways with some of the earliest lines appearing towards the beginning of the seventeenth century. At its peak in the mid-eighteenth century, the Tanfield Railway, which has been described earlier, and which led coal into Dunston from a wide

Dunston Staiths before refurbishment for the Gateshead Garden Festival.

Dunston Staiths working to full capacity in the early twentieth century.

area of northern Durham, carried more than half of all the coal shipped from Tyneside.

Dunston's pre-eminence in the transport of coal was such that one commentator described Dunston as 'the focal point of a transport system ...which remained unchallenged for a century and a half'. Gradually, however, from around 1770 onwards, new mining areas developed requiring different shipping points; the wagonways were progressively replaced by iron railways, dredging of the river and the replacement of the old Tyne Bridge meant that sea-going ships could come right up-river making keels and keelmen redundant, and Dunston's role as a coal transport centre gradually diminished.

Other Industries

As might be expected, Dunston tended to attract industrial concerns which were either involved in coal by-products like Norwood Cokeworks, Thomas Ness Tar Works and the Redheugh Gas Works, or manufactured products used in mining, wagonways and shipping like ropes (e.g. Bridon Fibres), iron products (e.g. Sir Ambrose Crowley's High Team Iron Works), plant and machinery (e.g. Dunston Engine Works) and ship-building (keels, yachts, wherries and racing boats). Towards the end of the nineteenth century, however, other industries were established, including the Dunston Flour Mills of the Co-operative Wholesale Society which were built in the late 1880s. These were an early example of reinforced concrete construction and were a popular place to work because they were lit by electricity. The CWS Soap Works were built on an adjoining site in 1909. Dunston A power station was built to the west of Dunston in 1910 and was replaced by the much larger Dunston B station in 1933, but the latter was demolished in 1986 and the site incorporated into the Metro Centre development.

A drawing of Dunston engine works, 1893.

CWS Flour Mills as they looked in 1978.

Dunston in the Nineteenth Century

A *History of Durham* by Mackenzie describes Dunston in 1843 as:

> a populous village in the Low-hand township. It stretches from the River Team westward along the margin of the Tyne for upwards of half a mile. The site seems to have been mostly gained from the River Tyne, and is therefore called 'The Bishop's Waste'. The houses, which are built with surprising irregularity, have mostly gardens attached to them. There are two or three neat and convenient houses, occupied by agents concerned in the coalworks, but most of the cottages are inhabited by keel-men.

He goes on to refer to the staiths and mentions the existence of timber yards, storehouses, a saw-mill, a candle factory, a coal-

An undated drawing of CWS Soap Works.

Dunston Power Station, from the air.

wagon wright, a keel-builder and four public houses. He also points out the existence of a smaller adjoining settlement at Cowheel containing a farmhold, two more public houses and a blacksmith's shop along with 'two very neat cottages'.

Mackenzie also describes the church school-room which had been opened in 1818 as 'large and commodious' and draws attention to the foundation stone attached to the gable-end which reads (it still exists today although the school is long since closed) 'Erected by Subscription Anno Domini 1818. The Hon. and Revd Edward Grey, Rector'. This was, of course, the Rector of Whickham as Dunston did not have its own Anglican church at this time. The Rector apparently subscribed £5 and other subscribers included the Bishop of Durham and a number of other people associated with Dunston. Each pupil had to pay at least 3d per week towards

the schoolmaster's stipend with any excess contributing to the building. Mackenzie comments that 'the poor man, under this strange arrangement, has actually paid upwards of £39. The school is at present in a very unprosperous state.'

Twenty-three years later, another *History of Durham* by Fordyce indicates that Dunston was developing quite quickly at this time because, in addition to the industries mentioned by Mackenzie he lists two chemical factories, a firebrick factory, two ship- and boat-building yards against Mackenzies' one, two spade and shovel makers, a licensed gunpowder magazine, and a brewery. Despite what must have been a significant increase in population, there were still only four public houses (a local directory of 1851 lists them as the Board, the Keel, the Highlander and the Cross Keys, with the Dun Cow being one of the two which Mackenzie noted as being at Cowheel) but these had now been joined by a beer-shop. The village had, however, acquired a police station and the Wesleyan, New Connection and Primitive Methodists each had a chapel. Fordyce also noted that 'the school is now conducted by a master and a mistress and is well attended'-clearly an improvement on 1834.

The King's Meadows

Dunston's Comprehensive school is called King's Meadow, the reference being to a flat green island of about thirty acres which used to be situated in the River Tyne at Dunston and which was known as King's Meadows. No one seems to know how the island acquired this name, although it has been suggested that at one time it may have belonged to the Castle in Newcastle and been used to grow food or fodder for the royal army.

There was a public house on the island known as the 'Countess of Coventry' reflecting a local link via a man called Thomas Moses. In the eighteenth century Moses, partly through native ability and partly as the result of marrying a series of rich ladies, became very wealthy and acquired extensive property including King's Meadows. His family married into the peerage, and it was his grand-daughter who eventually became the Countess of Coventry in the early nineteenth century and gave her name to the public house.

The island and the public house were apparently very quiet for most of the year, and the landlady used to keep cows as a sideline, taking the milk to the mainland each day by punt. This all changed on what were known as Barge Days when Newcastle Corporation used to sail their river boundaries in barges in the same way that many other places used to walk or ride their boundaries each year. On Barge Days, which took place annually up to 1850 and every five years thereafter, a fleet of barges, steam boats, keels, wherries and other craft led by the Mayor of Newcastle and the Master of Trinity House sailed up-river to the accompaniment of cannon fire, church bells and cheers from the crowd. Once the limit of their jurisdiction had been reached, they returned to King's Meadows for an afternoon of sport which included a rowing regatta and horse-racing as well as a variety of side-shows.

In the 1860s, the Tyne Commissioners decided to improve navigation on the river to enable sea-going vessels to sail up-river as far as Derwenthaugh. This meant that King's Meadows had to be removed. Dredging began in 1862 and was completed in 1887, so removing King's Meadows from the map and ending an interesting piece of Tyneside history.

Dunston Today
During the last 100 years, Dunston has changed enormously. It has continued to grow in size but, like Swalwell, has become increasingly a suburban area rather than an industrial one. It has also seen many dramatic changes.

The Team Valley Trading Estate, which was the first of the purpose-built industrial estates designed to attract industry to the area, is situated immediately to the east of Dunston and was opened by King George VI in 1939. Increasingly, however, it has become a commercial centre rather than an industrial one.

Other developments which affected both Swalwell and Dunston were the Western Bypass (now the A1) and the Metro Centre which were developed in the 1970s and 1980s and have had a considerable impact on life in both communities. One other development during the same period which had particular benefits for Dunston, however, was the removal of the Northern Clubs Federation Brewery (the brewery owned by clubs in the north of England on a co-operative basis) from Newcastle to a site in Dunston, east of the Metro Centre. The Gateshead National Garden Festival in 1990 which rehabilitated several areas of dereliction in the lower Team Valley also proved to be of great benefit to the image of the area, changing many people's perception of both Gateshead in general and Dunston in particular.

CHAPTER 6

Sunniside, Marley Hill and Byermoor

The area immediately to the south of Whickham village contains several communities which, like many others in County Durham, began life as agricultural villages, became centres of coal production and nowadays continue to exist primarily as residential suburbs of the Tyneside conurbation. This area was one of the 'quarters' of Whickham, and was given the name 'Fellside' from the hamlet which existed on Fellside Road midway between Whickham and Burnopfield. The name Fellside is self-explanatory as the hamlet, as it used to be, stands on the side of Whickham Fell, nearly 600ft above sea-level.

Fellside

Unlike the townships giving their names to the other three 'quarters' (Whickham village, Swalwell and Dunston), Fellside has diminished rather than grown in size over the years. Even one hundred years ago, it was a very small hamlet with only thirteen houses. A school, which had been financed by the Earl of Strathmore, had already closed by that time, but a Wesleyan chapel, built at the expense of another local benefactor, was then still in existence but is now also long gone. Apart from the few houses and local farms which still exist in the vicinity, the main buildings at Fellside today are the Woodman's Arms, a public house which is upwards of 200 years old, albeit much modernized, and the East Byermoor Guest House occupying former farm buildings.

Byermoor

Byermoor is a very old village which is mentioned in the *Boldon Book*. There are two explanations of the origin of the name. One suggests that it comes from Biermore or Beechemoor meaning 'Bare moor', the other that it was originally 'Beaghere's moor' presumably meaning the moor belonging to Beaghere. It is certainly high on the fell which makes 'moor' appropriate, but there does not seem to be any justification for attempts to rationalize the spelling into 'Byremoor' (presumably meaning 'the moor with a cow-shed') even though William Bourn, the

Victorian local historian, used this version throughout his history of Whickham.

Several well-known local families have played a part in the history of Byermoor. In the fourteenth century, Byermoor belonged to the de-Guildefords, but in the fifteenth century it passed by marriage into the possession of the Hodgeson family who subsequently sold it on to the Harrisons. A Harrison descendant married into the Harding family of Hollinside with the result that Byermoor passed into the hands of the Bowes family in 1730 along with the rest of the Hollinside estate.

Coal-mining was carried on at Byermoor for much of this time but a modern shaft was sunk in the mid-nineteenth century. This resulted in progressively increased production over the years, notwithstanding the closure of the battery of beehive coke ovens on the site before the First World War. The colliery was finally closed in 1968. Originally, Byermoor itself consisted of colliery houses built in the second half of the nineteenth century, but after the Second World War these were demolished and replaced by modern housing, sadly enough to coincide with the closure of the colliery which gave the village its reason for existence.

Perhaps the village's most significant buildings today are Byermoor Sacred Heart Church, opened in 1876, and the adjoining school, opened in 1883. These were originally built, in part at least, to serve the adjoining community of Burnopfield which became part of a separate local authority following local government reorganisation in 1974. Fortunately, Gateshead Education Authority intervened to ensure that the church and school could continue to serve their planned role.

Marley Hill

Like Byermoor, there is more than one explanation for the origin of the name Marley Hill. One suggests that Marley means 'a clearing near a boundary' with Hill as a later addition. An alternative explanation is that the name is derived from the de Merley family who owned the area in the twelfth century. It may be, of course, that the first explanation is the correct one and that the de Marleys (meaning 'of Merley') took their name from the place rather than the other way round.

In the sixteenth century, Elizabeth Marley (the 'de' had gone by this time and the spelling had changed slightly) married into the Blakiston family, and a subsequent marriage meant that Marley Hill, along with Gibside itself, subsequently passed into the hands of the Bowes family.

A map of Marley Hill as it was in 1898.

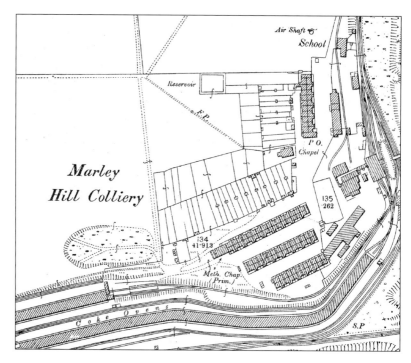

Marley Hill coke ovens.

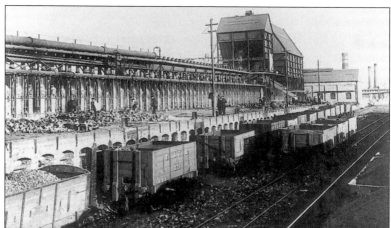

This area was an excellent example of early mining countryside where agriculture existed alongside coal-mining for many centuries. Bourn, writing in the 1890s, states, 'A great number of coalpits have been worked here, some of them centuries ago. Anyone looking at the map of the Ordnance Survey, will see the district dotted with "shaft". In the books belonging to the Gibside estate, there are fifty-eight pits – all named – mentioned as working in the year 1724'. Despite this intensive coal-mining activity – mainly in the form of fairly shallow bell-pits, of course – Bourn goes on to say that 'Seventy years ago [i.e. in the 1820s, 100 years after the date

Chapel Row, Marley Hill. The chapel from which the road takes its name is visible at the far end of the row.

of the Gibside entries], the district was all moorland, and with the exception of a farm house, no dwelling was to be seen.'

Despite Bourn's reference to the absence of surface buildings, deep mining in the area seems to have begun around the middle of the eighteenth century and, apart from a break of about twenty-five years in the early nineteenth century when it was temporarily abandoned as unprofitable, continued until Marley Hill colliery finally closed in 1983.

Sunniside and Streetgate

Interestingly, Sunniside, which is now by far the biggest of the communities to the immediate south of Whickham, was the last to develop as such, although it has an equally long history. At one time it formed part of the Gibside estate when this was in the hands of the Blakiston family, but it subsequently changed hands many times over the centuries. The name is generally accepted to be derived from a Saxon chief called Sunna with the 'side' having its conventional North East meaning of 'slope' or 'hill'. In the thirteenth century, a large part of modern Sunniside belonged to a man called Gilbert or Gilly Gategang and his brother, and was known as Gilly's Meadow which eventually became Gellesfield, a name familiar to local people but now only preserved in Gellesfield Chare, a road on Grange Estate in Whickham. Gellesfield Hole, however, once the site of a colliery, is still remembered in Hole Lane.

A local family with the Marley Hill Colliery banner at the annual Durham Miners' Gala.

There is no generally accepted explanation of the name of Streetgate, to the north-east of Sunniside, but it may be derived from 'straight-gate' meaning 'straight road' to describe a straight section of the main road which is otherwise fairly twisting.

Apart from a few buildings in the centre of the village, most of modern Sunniside is a twentieth century creation. The oldest part of the village, appropriately known as Old Sunniside, was

*Sunniside village centre,
early twentieth century.*

centred on Old Sunniside Farm, a seventeenth century farm, but
the surrounding eighteenth century houses were demolished in the
mid-1930s and replaced by council housing.

Mention must be made of the Sunniside Social Club. As in many
other northern communities, including Whickham, Swalwell and
Dunston, much of the social life of the community revolves round
'the club'. Sunniside, however, has a particular claim to fame
because two members of the club committee, Victor Dillon, club
chairman, and Bill Liddle, club secretary, have served on the board
of the Federation Brewery, Vic Dillon serving as board chairman
from 1974 until his death in 1984.

*The road from Sunniside
to Whickham.*

CHAPTER 7

Whickham Parish Church

Structure of the Church

The oldest surviving building in Whickham is the Parish church of St Mary the Virgin, part of which is Norman, dating from the early twelfth century. There was probably an earlier church on the site but no record of this, or the early history of the present church, now exists. An approximate history of the present building can, however, be derived from the differing architectural styles reflected in the various sections of the surviving structure.

The present church probably began as what is known as a 'two-cell' church consisting of a nave and sanctuary. Around 100 years later, in the Early English period, a more elaborate structure was added, with north and south aisles. These were reconstructed during the Decorated period of the fourteenth century, and a porch and tower were added at about the same time. The tower was originally 47ft high, but a 6ft parapet was added in the fifteenth century which raised the overall height to 53ft. The porch was subsequently destroyed in the 'Great Storm' of November 1703 and had to be rebuilt using the same stones. A disastrous fire in 1841 required an extensive amount of restoration work which was not completed until 1862 when the opportunity was taken to add

How Whickham Parish church may have looked in Cromwell's time.

Dunston West Farm on Whickham Highway, a Grade II listed building dating from the mid-eighteenth century, which is now Whickham Riding School. Traces of early mine workings and wagonways can be seen in the fields behind the riding school.

Looking east along Whickham Highway. The houses on the right, some of which are Grade II listed buildings, date from the seventeenth and eighteenth centuries and include Beech House, at one time a boys' school, attended by the future Lord Armstrong and a future distinguished Rector of Whickham, the Revd Henry Byne Carr.

Early nineteenth-century rubble stone cottages, in Duckpool Lane, now extensively modernized.

The Orchard in spring, making an attractive entrance to the village.

Cottage at the corner of Dockendale Lane, which may have been an eighteenth-century toll house.

Dockendale Hall, where Cromwell is reputed to have stayed when he passed through Whickham in the mid-seventeenth century.

Whickham Lodge, one of Whickham's eighteenth-century mansions and listed Grade II, used to be surrounded by nineteen acres of parkland, now largely covered with modern housing.

Another group of rubble stone cottages, also listed as Grade II, facing the foot of Broom Lane and probably dating from the eighteenth century. Wesley is believed to have preached outside these cottages in 1752.

Spring blossom in Whickham Chase Park.

Whickham Chase Park, with Whickham House, since demolished, appearing to the left of the picture.

The mill in Whickham Chase Park which gave Millfield Road its name. The age of this particular building is unknown but there is a reference in parish records to a mill which probably stood on this site as early as 1567 and the surviving building, listed Grade II, was still working well into the nineteenth century.

Whickham Park, another of Whickham's Grade II listed buildings, was the residence of Charles Attwood, the well-known radical, in the nineteenth century. It is now divided into four separate dwellings.

The Knowles, with the original Parochial school, opened in 1742, and the School House facing the camera.

The former Whickham Council Offices, dating from 1904.

Park Cottage in School Lane dates from 1791, and was originally two cottages occupied by the head gardener and coachman from Whickham Park.

The Parish Church of St Mary the Virgin is partly Norman and is a Grade I listed building. It is the oldest building in Whickham still in use.

The memorial to William Shield, the musician and composer, in Whickham churchyard.

The stone on the railing in front of the church recording the preservation of the Church Green by the Revd Henry Byne Carr and his brother Ralph Carr-Ellison in 1852.

The former coach house which was used by the Clavering family when attending church is now a baker's shop.

The Rectory, dating from the sixteenth century, is the oldest surviving residence in the village.

The old Coach House, which has served a wide variety of uses over the centuries and is now a fitness

The Village Tea Rooms, which were originally a tithe barn.

Rose Villa, the home of the late Dr Andrew (Dr Andy) Smith whose family served the community as doctors for over a century.

The monument to John (Lang Jack) English, the one-time leader of 'Crowley's Crew' which was re-erected here after it was vandalized in its original position. The public house behind, formerly the Rose and Crown, has since been re-named Ye Olde Lang Jack in his honour.

St Mary's Green, a modern shopping
area, developed in the 1970s and 1980s.
The green board to the right refers to
Whickham's regular successes in the annual
Britain in Bloom awards.

The Spoor Memorial chapel, named in
honour of Joseph Spoor, who rose from
working on the keels as a boy to become a
minister and noted preacher.

Whickham Salerooms, originally built as a Miners' Welfare Hall and adapted to their present purpose in 1966.

The stones of the former Village Pump built into the wall in front of the Glebe housing estate.

Salisbury House, one of a number of attractive old houses on the south side of Front Street which are listed Grade II.

The Hermitage, built in 1790 by Matthew Taylor, owner of Swalwell Brewery. It is now used as a council residential home.

Whickham Community Centre, initially a medical centre and later a colliery institute, became a community centre after the Axwell Park Colliery closed in 1953.

A Victorian post-box still serving its purpose outside the Community Centre.

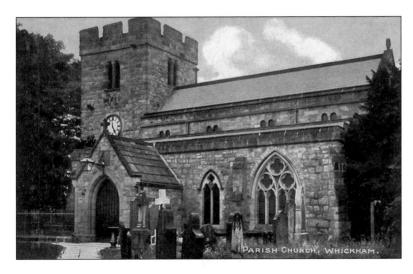

Whickham parish church in the twentieth century.

a second north aisle. The earliest surviving parts of the church are the chancel arch, the three pillars forming the arcade of the south aisle, the font and the tower.

The chancel arch is one of the few examples in the north of England of true Norman work, because most claimed Norman architecture dates from the late twelfth century, i.e. in Plantagenet times, and is strictly speaking 'transitional' (between Norman and Early English) in style. The arch is semi-circular with two square orders, both slightly chamfered, and rests on scalloped cushion capitals. These are of slightly different design, which is typical of early Norman building.

The chancel is part of the original fabric and retains a number of interesting features although the lighting was altered during the restoration of 1862. The altar dates from the seventeenth century after the original stone altar was destroyed by the Puritans.

The nave is Norman with clerestory windows. The plastered areas of the walls may have been decorated with murals which were a common method of teaching Bible stories when most people were illiterate. The pillars of the south aisle may also have been coloured.

Other noteworthy features include the baptistery containing the font, made of Stanhope marble, the porch containing two fourteenth century grave covers set into the west wall and a 1651 sundial over the entrance, and the tower which contains six bells of which one was originally cast in 1657 but recast in 1854, and two others date from 1745 and 1775 respectively.

The church contains a number of monuments, including several to former Rectors and members of the Carr family of Dunston Hill who were great benefactors of the church.

Parish Records

The earliest existing parish records begin about the middle of the sixteenth century, with the earliest inventory dating from 1553, baptisms and burials from 1576 and marriages from 1579. There may have been earlier records but if so they no longer exist. Among the most striking entries to modern eyes are references to people having 'perished in the snow' on a number of occasions, and deaths from the plague in 1610, 1626, 1644 and 1646, because they seem so alien to life in modern Whickham. In some ways, however, entries concerning more mundane matters are more significant, reflecting as they do the much greater role which the Church played in the broader life of the community in the past, serving not only as the religious centre of the community but as its social and political centre also.

As in other parts of the country prior to the Local Government Acts of the nineteenth century, many of the functions which we nowadays associate with the local authority were carried out by the churchwardens in collaboration with the 'four and twenty'. The latter body was a form of self-appointed 'select

The Rectory, or Whickham Hall, is a sixteenth century building and probably the oldest surviving residence in the village. It ceased to be the Rectory in 1713 but was restored to its original function in 1922.

This building was purpose-built as a Rectory in 1713 and continued to serve this purpose until 1922. It was subsequently used as a Cottage Hospital for many years before being converted to other uses. This photograph shows the arms of Lord Crewe, Bishop of Durham, still visible over the entrance.

vestry' consisting of the more affluent members of local society, co-opting members up to a generally agreed number (hence the 'four and twenty') which made many decisions on behalf of the wider community.

The financing of the church was an obvious duty of the churchwardens and one early record required every person having seats in the church to pay 2s 6d per seat towards church repairs. An 'Easter reckoning' was also levied to pay the Rector. At the end of the seventeenth century, this was 1 ½ d per person over sixteen years of age plus 1d per chimney plus 4d per hen-house and so on through a series of charges for sheep, cows, geese, turkeys, pigs and ducks. Even bees were not exempt, with charges ranging from 4d per swarm for those with fewer than five swarms to 1s 4d per swarm for the Rector (presumably reflecting his greater affluence). Non-religious duties included poor-relief for which the churchwardens could levy a Poor Rate and records of this exist from 1677 when the first entry begins 'The names of ye Pishoners of Whickham for their Cesse [i.e. rate] for ye poore for ye yeare 1677.' Other duties included finding orphans a trade (Oliver Twist comes to mind), looking after old people and burying paupers. Other entries are concerned with the destruction of dogs to keep down rabies, and the rates paid to parishioners killing animals defined as vermin – 1s for a fox's head, 8d for a badger's head and 4d for a foumart's (wild-cat's) head.

Some of the more entertaining entries from the Churchwardens' Book in the later eighteenth century include:

1760 Paid for ringing the bells on hearing Quebec was taken	2s 0d
1773 Paid for a new pair of stocks	12s 0d
1775 Paid for drinks for the masons	£1 5s 2d
1789 Paid for tobacco for the workhouse	2s 3d
To a charge for a dinner for the Church-wardens on the Thanksgiving for the King's recovery	10s 0d

Rectors of Whickham

There is a list of rectors (or vicars – the titles are not used consistently) of Whickham displayed on a wall in the church, the first being Alan around AD 1200. Others worthy of note are:

1313: Robert de Baldock, who became Bishop of Norwich, and Lord Chancellor;

1635: Thomas Wood, who became chaplain to King Charles I, and Bishop of Coventry and Lichfield;

1685: William Graham, who became Dean of Carlisle and later Wells, and chaplain to Princess Anne of Denmark;

1712: Dr Robert Thomlinson, who was Prebendary of St Paul's Cathedral and was responsible for building Whickham Parochial school; (a fuller account of his career and contribution to the life of Whickham is given in the history of Whickham Parochial school below);

1816: The Hon. Edward Grey, who became Dean and then Bishop of Hereford;

1829: Henry Liddell, grandfather of the Alice Liddell who became the Alice of *Alice in Wonderland*;

1846: Henry Byne Carr, who served for fifty years (the longest serving Rector), set up new churches in Dunston, Marley Hill and Swalwell and was responsible, with his brother Ralph Carr-Ellison, for the restoration of the church after the 1841 fire and for preserving the village green for the community.

In 1650, under the Commonwealth, Cuthbert Stote, a Puritan, was installed as minister and remained in possession until the restoration of Charles II. In 1660 he 'surrendered' the Rectory 'into the hands and possession of Dr Thomas Wood, Chaplain in Ordinary to his late Majesty, who was injuriously put out of the said living: It is ordered by the Lords in Parliament assembled, that the said Dr Wood be and is hereby restored to the said Rectory and the said Cuthbert Stote is discharged from the said Rectory accordingly'. Cuthbert Stote is subsequently recorded as an 'Intruder'.

The Churchyard

The churchyard contains many interesting graves. The oldest is on the south side of the church and contains the remains of Mary Pescod who died on fourteenth February 1609, but there are other very old tombs in this part of the churchyard including those of Jane Jackson who died in 1620 and Doruthie Grages who died in 1632. Cromwell's passage through the village in 1648 and 1650 are also recalled from the deaths which are recorded in the Parish Register as 'A souldier to L-General Cromwell. 1648' and 'Richard Claydon, a souldier to Coll. Wylde, 31 [sic] September 1650'. There were also a surprising number of centenarians buried in the eighteenth and early nineteenth centuries – eight were buried between 1724 and 1826 (four men and four women) ranging in age from 100 to 105. In the absence of accurate records, of course, it is always possible that at least some of these cases are really the result of old people exaggerating their longevity.

Two stones to the north of the tower mark the graves of George and Abia Hodgson, Quakers, who died in 1667 and 1669 respectively and, presumably for religious reasons, were originally buried in a field at the west end of the village, but were reburied here in 1784. The graves of notable local residents, whose contributions to the history of Whickham are described elsewhere, include the family vault of the Carrs of Dunston Hill which is to the west of the porch, and a stone commemorating the Hardings of Hollinside to the north side of the church. Also to the north of the church is the stone erected to the memory of J.J. 'Jacky' Robinson, probably the most famous headmaster of Whickham Parochial school, who died in 1874, aged seventy-four years. Near the entrance to the churchyard from Church Chare there is a monument to the memory of William Shield which reads 'In memory of William Shield, musician and composer; born at Swalwell, 5 March, 1748; died in London, 25 January, 1829; buried in Westminster Abbey. Erected by public subscription, 1891.' Perhaps the most imposing memorial, however, is that erected to the memory of Harry Clasper, the famous Tyneside oarsman.

Church Green

In front of the church is the church green which nowadays presents an attractive and colourful centre for the village. Although, like other village greens, it has had a long history, it did not always present such a pleasant picture. After the Rebellion of the Northern Earls in 1569, two of the rebels were probably executed on the village green and the village stocks were almost

THE VILLAGE GREEN, WHICKHAM.

The church and village green as they probably looked in Atkins' time.

certainly sited on the village green also. One of its pleasanter later functions, however, was to serve as a playground for the pupils of the Parochial school.

In 1851, a man called William Atkins claimed ownership of the Church Green, quoting a 'Deed of Feoffment dated 1795' (an archaic form of land transfer) and the leases of 'two closes called Garths before the Church'. Although at first sight, such a claim on ancient public land might seem absurd, it should be remembered that it was a period of enclosures (the 500 acres of Whickham Fell had been enclosed as recently as 1811) and the church green was apparently described as 'undistributed waste land' in the Whickham Enclosure map of 1811 and the Tithe map of 1840. In the course of pursuing his claim Atkins cut down a number of trees, closed a footpath across the green, enclosed it with wooden rails and by the end of the year had dug 'large holes in the Green and altered it very much' and had 'covered one of the roads with rubbish'. The villagers were outraged and reacted by destroying the fence, threatening Atkins, and carrying an effigy of him round the village. In January 1852 Atkins was actually arrested and jailed briefly. A long process of negotiation followed with Atkins trying to achieve a compromise but a meeting with an arbitrator finally took place on 2 August 1852, probably at the Bay Horse, with judgement being finally given on 14 September 1852. The then Rector, Revd Henry Byne Carr, persuaded his brother, Ralph Carr-Ellison of Dunston Hill, to buy the green so that it could be preserved for the use of the people of Whickham for all time.

These events are commemorated on a stone slab on the north side of the green which reads (although the inscription is now badly corroded):

In 1852 owing to the efforts of the Revd H.B. Carr, Rector of this parish for 50 years 1846-1896, and of his Brother, Ralph Carr-Ellison, of Dunston Hill, this Church Green was preserved for the use of the People of Whickham for all time and vested in the Rector and Churchwardens as the Lawful Custodians.

Despite this generous gesture, the green remained a fairly unimpressive area with a surface of clay and hardcore rather than grass, which was used every May as the site of the village hoppings. This ended in 1935 when, after a very wet week of poor takings, the showmen refused to pay their usual rent and the Rector banned them from the site permanently. With the steadily increasing volume of vehicular traffic, the green was thereafter used more and more as a car park.

In 1953, Whickham Urban District Council agreed to take over responsibility for the site, and proceeded to landscape it and maintain its grass and flowers to a high standard. This arrangement has been continued by Gateshead Metropolitan Borough Council, and the green now forms an attractive focal point for the village and plays a major role in securing regular awards for Whickham in the annual Britain in Bloom competitions.

The green as it looked before the council assumed responsibility for its upkeep.

Speculum Gregis

Before taking our leave of the parish church and reviewing the history of other churches in the area, mention should be made of a document known as the *Speculum Gregis of Whickham Parish, Durham, 1835* or 'Mirror of the Flock'. This is a hand-written document prepared by W. Gould, curate at the time, but there is no indication of the reason for its preparation, whether it was merely a personal investigation or part of some more wide-ranging project. It consists of a list of every household in the parish, giving the name, occupation, religion and educational background of the householder, together with the place of marriage and the numbers of sons, daughters, servants and lodgers. A final column contains 'Remarks' which are frequently less than complimentary.

Many of the surnames listed are still familiar ones in the area today, and in the light of some of the entries in the 'Remarks' column, it is probably better not to list them here, but the occupations given are very interesting as a comment on the class structure of the day. A sample of the entries for Whickham itself indicates that more than a quarter of the population either had private means, being described as 'independent' or 'esquire', or were in the professional classes (clergy, medicine and education). At the time, Whickham was clearly on the way towards being a fairly affluent residential area. At the other end of the scale, however, 10 per cent of the population were described simply as 'paupers' with some being further described as 'very poor', but the same description was also added to some of those shown as being in employment. In between these two extremes, about a quarter of the population were keelmen, reflecting the area's continuing involvement in the shipment of coal, another quarter tradesmen, skilled craftsmen and shopkeepers and 10 per cent engaged in farming and allied pursuits (farmers, countrymen, gardeners, grooms, etc.). Of the remainder, it is interesting to note that very few were associated with mining itself, presumably reflecting the shift of mining southwards from Whickham.

The religions are given as Churchman (meaning Church of England), Methodist, Wesleyan, Presbyterian, Primitive Methodist (alternatively described as Ranters), and Roman Catholic, but the author of the document goes on to classify the degree of commitment in each case, indicating whether the members of each family were regular attenders at church, regular attenders at any house of worship, attenders at either Communion or Mass, were able to read, possessed a bible and/or prayer book, and whether family prayers were said. As might be expected at that date, a very high proportion of the population were members of, and regular attenders at, the Church of England, although there was a fair sprinkling of Free Church members, especially in Swalwell. What is perhaps more surprising at that date is the very large number who were literate and possessed both a bible and a prayer book.

So far as education is concerned, the majority had had no school education at all (which makes the level of literacy even more remarkable), and of those who had attended school, most had gone to a private school rather than a National school, with a few whose only schooling was Sunday school. This probably reflects the availability or otherwise of educational facilities in the area rather than any personal preferences, because the places of marriage would suggest that most householders came from Whickham itself, where virtually the only school available was the Parochial school, or from the surrounding areas where facilities were often much worse.

Turning to the Remarks section, it seems apparent that many of these were intended either for the eyes of the author only, or for at most a very restricted circle. Sample entries are:

Bears a bad character in the neighbourhood (about a keelman).
Humble and pious (a frequent phrase).
Wishes to do what is right (another favourite phrase).
Very ill, penitent and humble (apparently a single parent).
Drinks much, wife professes much, is very bitter against the church.
Pharisaical beyond measure (a pauper).
Professes more than practices (a countryman).
House and family bad name (a publican).
Freethinker, believes only part of bible (a smith).
Pharisaical and impudent (another keelman).
Very ignorant (and another).

Altogether it is a fascinating document. One can imagine the reception which would be given today to a modern census-taker making these sorts of enquiries.

CHAPTER 8

Other Churches

Church of England

The parish church is by far the oldest church in the village, dating back, as it does, about 900 years, and in consequence it has played a major role in the history of the community. It was the only Anglican church in the area, serving not only Whickham itself, but Swalwell, Dunston and Marley Hill until the second half of the nineteenth century when Revd Henry Byne Carr, one of the Carrs of Dunston Hill and Whickham's longest serving Rector (1846-1896), initiated the division of the old parish into its four quarters and set up new churches in Dunston (Christ church) in 1873, Marley Hill (St Cuthbert's) in 1877 and Swalwell (Holy Trinity) in 1894. Sadly, Christ church, in Dunston, had to be closed because of subsidence in 1976 and was demolished shortly thereafter.

Christ church, Dunston, 1873-1976.

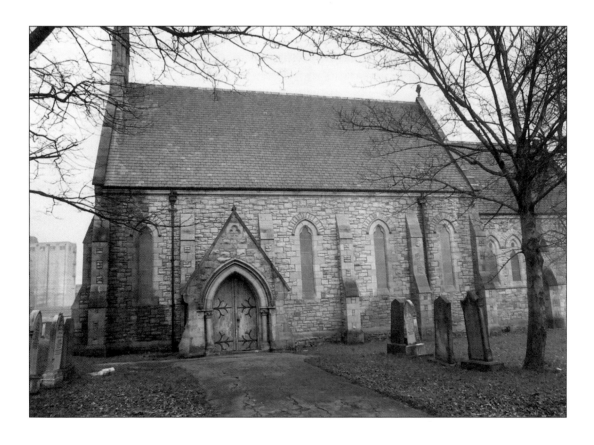

Fortunately, another church, St Nicholas', had been opened in 1964 to serve the southern part of the original Dunston parish.

Reformation

From Tudor times onwards, however, the single 'national' church which had existed since medieval times began to fragment as part of the process generally known as the Reformation. Some background to this and the emergence of the dissenting churches may be helpful here before considering the impact on Whickham.

Attempts to reform the Roman Catholic Church for religious reasons had begun as early as the twelfth century but only gathered momentum in the sixteenth century when the absolute rulers of the day began to use their increasing power to undermine the political influence and wealth of the Church. In consequence, the religious and political aspects of the Reformation are often confused. In this country, the changes are usually associated with the 'break with Rome' and the dissolution of the monasteries in the reign of Henry VIII, but these were essentially political changes rather than religious ones, with the sovereign replacing the Pope as head of a church which, at the time, remained Catholic in most of its observances, although seen as Protestant by the Roman Catholics.

The important religious changes took place only slowly over a much longer period. After Henry's son Edward had tried to move the church towards more strictly Protestant religious practices, and his daughter Mary had tried to reverse that process, his third child, Elizabeth, wisely adopted a policy of conciliation, attempting to reconcile the views of the reformers and the traditionalists within the single 'broad church' which the Church of England remains today.

Many of the great landowners in the area around Whickham were Roman Catholic but Whickham itself belonged to a member of the Clavering family who was a Puritan, and it was claimed that by the middle of the seventeenth century there was not a single Roman Catholic living in Whickham. It was about the same time, in 1650 under the Commonwealth, that Cuthbert Stote, a Puritan, was 'intruded' as Rector, only to be removed following the restoration of the monarchy in 1662.

Presbyterianism

Following the ejection of Cuthbert Stote and other Puritan/Presbyterian ministers (thirty-eight in Northumberland and eighteen in Durham) in 1662, Presbyterianism became illegal

for a time, but was allowed to function openly under the Act of Indulgence of 1672 and finally achieved full freedom in 1688 following the accession of William of Orange and Mary.

Locally, the congregation was drawn from a very wide area and originally met at Ryton Woodside, but in 1750 a new chapel, the Ebenezer Chapel, was opened for services in Swalwell and served the community for over two centuries until it finally had to be demolished in 1976. However, the foundation stone has been preserved and used to mark the site. Services were subsequently held in premises immediately opposite the site of the original church.

Margaret Dryburgh

Perhaps the best-known name associated with the Ebenezer Chapel is that of Margaret Dryburgh. Her father was William Dryburgh, a native of North Northumberland, who started his working life as a farmer and became a Presbyterian minister relatively late in life. He became the minister at the Ebenezer Chapel in 1887 and remained there until his retirement in 1906. He is remembered both for his work with young people and for initiating the building of a replacement for the original Ebenezer Chapel building which dated from 1750. Margaret Dryburgh was born in 1890 and her formative years were spent in Swalwell. Her father's example led her to become a missionary and in 1939 she was working in the Far East when the Second World War broke out. She was captured by the Japanese in 1942 and held in captivity until, tragically, she died shortly before the end of the war in 1945. During her time as a prisoner, she used

The bottom of Napier Road, Swalwell, c. 1900. The Ebenezer Chapel is straight ahead, with the Presbyterian church at the foot of the road on the left-hand side and the entrance to the Primitive Methodist chapel on the right. The winding gear of the Henry Pit is faintly visible in the distance.

SWALWELL.

her considerable musical talents in a variety of ways to maintain morale among her fellow prisoners. A film, *Paradise Road*, has been made about her life, and two wards at Dunston Hill Hospital have been named after her.

John Wesley and Methodism

John Wesley was ordained in the Church of England in 1728, but became converted to evangelical work in 1738 and spent the next fifty years riding throughout the country on horseback preaching in the open air. He visited Whickham twice, in 1742 and 1752. On his first visit in 1742 Wesley seems not to have been impressed with his reception. He records in his Journal:

> *Between twelve and one I preached in a convenient ground at Whickham… I spoke strong, rough words, but I did not perceive that any regarded what was spoken… I left them, very well content with the preacher and with themselves.*

He was more specific in his comment on preaching at Tanfield two days later:

> *So dead, senseless, unaffected a congregation I scarce have seen, except at Whickham.*

On his second visit to Whickham, in 1752, Wesley records that he preached 'before Mrs Armstrong's door' which is believed to be one of the cottages adjoining Whickham Garage in Front Street. He also visited Swalwell three times – in 1747, 1757 and 1759 – apparently receiving a friendlier reception than he had in Whickham. In 1759, the room in which he was due to preach would hold only a third of the people who wished to hear him and the Presbyterian minister offered him the use of the Ebenezer Chapel, which was accepted.

Despite Wesley's reservations about Whickham, however, Methodism acquired a considerable following in the area, as it did elsewhere in the Durham coalfield, probably for a mixture of reasons. On the negative side, there was a tendency to associate the Church of England with the ruling classes, in particular the mine-owners (the view that the Church of England is 'the Conservative Party at prayer' has a long history). In addition, the rector himself was often related to the local gentry and was also fairly affluent in his own right putting him squarely on the side of the employers. On the positive side Methodism offered

*The former West End
Wesleyan church,
Whickham, which was
built in 1869.*

a down-to earth, more informal, more 'working-class' approach
to religion encouraging self-respect and, in the days before the
wide availability of education, the chance to learn to read, to
speak in public and to join in community activity.

It should also be remembered, of course, that until the
second half of the nineteenth century there was only one
parish church serving the whole of the area and the *Speculum
Gregis* suggests that the proportion of the population declaring
themselves to be Methodists was lower in the area around the
church in Whickham itself than in the more distant Swalwell,
Dunston and Marley Hill. It is possible that this 'competition'
from the Methodists was a factor leading to the establishment
of new Anglican churches in those areas. In the early days,
however, there were quite friendly relations between the
Anglicans and the Methodists. Indeed, after their founding in
1739 the Methodists initially remained within the Church of
England and only became a separate body in 1795. In 1835,
the *Speculum Gregis* still showed twenty-six families which
claimed to be both church and chapel, and in 1840 one man
was both parish clerk in the church and singing master in
the chapel. Later still, when the Primitive Methodist Church
inaugurated their Sunday school, it was the Rector, the Revd
Henry Byne Carr, who presented the bibles and testaments to
the superintendent and teachers for the use of the school.

Primitive Methodism

Like all radical movements, methodism showed a tendency to fragment, and doctrinal divisions led to groups breaking away from the original (Wesleyan) Methodists and setting up their own meeting places throughout the nineteenth century. This usually resulted in a large number of meeting places with relatively small congregations. Locally, however, the Primitive Methodists, who wished to preserve the Wesleyan practice of open-air preaching through camp meetings (hence 'the Ranters'), became particularly strong, as indicated in the *Speculum Gregis*.

These divisions were finally ended in 1932 when the various strands of Methodism were re-united in a single Methodist Church.

Spoor Memorial Methodist Church

It would be inappropriate in this general history to try to incorporate a comprehensive survey of all the methodist churches which have existed in the area over the years, but one particular church deserves a special mention – the Spoor Memorial Methodist church in Front Street which commemorates the life of a remarkable man. This church was named after Joseph Spoor who was born in Whickham on 2 June 1813. He received some rudimentary education at Whickham National schools but his father died very young and Joseph was removed from school and set to work on the keels so that he could contribute to the family budget. In 1829, he came under the influence of the Revd Hodgson Casson and despite the lack of both books and money, he began to take an active interest in Methodism, initially with the Wesleyan Methodist Society in Whickham and then with the Primitive Methodists, becoming a minister and a popular travelling preacher. By the time of his death in 1866, he had risen from working as a keelman to being probably the most successful minister in the Primitive Methodist church.

The Spoor Memorial Methodist Church opened in 1871 as a Primitive Methodist church and continues as a Methodist church today.

Roman Catholicism

Although some of the great landowners in the area were Roman Catholics, they found it prudent to keep a low profile following the religious troubles of the sixteenth and seventeenth centuries, and it was not until the second half of the nineteenth century that Roman Catholicism began to re-emerge in the area. Interestingly,

The Spoor Memorial Methodist church, originally built as a Primitive Methodist chapel in 1871.

whereas Anglicanism had had its historical focus in Whickham and had spread outwards from there, Roman Catholicism followed a reverse process and circled through the surrounding areas before finally establishing itself in Whickham village. Services were first held in Byermoor in 1869 which led to the consecration of Sacred Heart Church in that village in 1876. The second church to be opened was St Philip Neri, Dunston, in 1882 after which there was a lull in building although priests from Blaydon began conducting services in the Co-operative Society hall in Swalwell in 1922. It was not until the Second World War that priests from St Philip Neri began conducting services in Whickham and this

The former stables of Dockendale Hall were extensively altered in 1948 to serve as the Roman Catholic church of St Mary's, Whickham until a new church could be built.

led to a decision to set up a proper church in Whickham as soon as conditions permitted.

In 1948, the church authorities bought Dockendale Hall and adapted it to serve as the presbytery, with the former stables being extensively altered to serve as the Church of St Mary's, Dockendale. Although alterations were made over the following years, the growing population eventually necessitated the building of a completely new church and presbytery in the grounds which opened in 1973. Dockendale Hall has since been converted into flats and the former stables are now the church hall.

CHAPTER 9

Education

Earliest School

The first school in the Whickham area was set up in Swalwell by Ambrose Crowley in the early eighteenth century. This appears to have been situated in Quality Row, Swalwell and was fairly small. No trace of it now remains.

Whickham Parochial School

The next school to be set up was Whickham Parochial school which was established in 1714 by the then rector, Robert Thomlinson, and is the oldest surviving school in Whickham. It is probably fair to say that Dr Thomlinson was both a great rector and a great benefactor of Whickham. He was born in 1668 in Cumberland, obtained his BA in 1685 at the age of seventeen, his MA in 1692 and had served as rector in Somerset and as vicar of Eglingham in Northumberland before coming to Whickham in 1712. He obtained his Doctorate in Divinity in 1719. When he was installed as Rector of Whickham, he apparently found the church in a rather dilapidated state because within a short period of time he restored the chancel, installed a new clock in the tower, built a new porch, and erected galleries in the north and south aisles. He also laid the foundation stone of the new rectory in Rectory Lane in 1713. His main contribution to the life of the village, however, was undoubtedly the founding of what was originally

Whickham Parochial school, opened in 1714.

called the Whickham Charity School. In 1711, Mrs Jane Blakiston of Gibside bequeathed £100 to be used for the purpose of teaching the poor children of the parish the Church Catechism, reading and writing and for putting the boys out to a trade, and it was with this legacy together with additional funding provided by himself that Dr Thomlinson founded the school in 1714. It was recorded in the archives of the Society for the Propagation of Christian Knowledge in 1715 that 'a Gentlewoman of Whickham having left £100 to that Parish, appointing the Rector and Churchwardens to lay out the interest in teaching poor children, has induced (the Rector) to erect a Charity school there for 36 children at his own charge, to read, write and cast accounts, opened 19th October last'. Over the years, other local residents who left land and money in trust for the school included Robert Marshall, Thomas Bowes, George Bowes and John Huett.

From the beginning, there were economic pressures which caused problems in securing the attendance of poor children at school as a letter from Dr Thomlinson a few years later records:

The labour of loading coals by wagons is so great as usually to bring the men to their graves in the middle of their age, which fills the neighbouring parishes full of poor widows and children, the maintenance of whom chiefly depends upon the labour of the children, who are commonly employed either in the pits or in leading carts in the summer time from 6 or 7 years old. So that if their attendance at school should be rigorously demanded the poor families would starve, and therefore all that can be done is to prevail with those that live near the school to come part of the day when they have left their work.

Although the school had opened in 1714, it was not until 1742 that the building was completely finished, as recorded on a stone on the south side of the building and as recorded in a letter to the SPCK in that year when the school had 100 pupils including the 36 poor children. The letter states:

I have finished the Church School here [Whickham] after the plan of one I had built at Wigton in Cumberland, in which Parish I was born. It is a handsome stone building, nineteen yards in length. The front is ashlar work. The school about twelve yards in length, at the end of which is a staircase, a parlour, two closets, a kitchen, and milk-house all below. Above are five lodging rooms. There are behind it a garden, a cowhouse with some conveniences. It stands in a good air and has a pleasant prospect. The master is obliged to teach thirty-six poor children. The endowment arises chiefly from the profits of two galleries, which I have erected in the Parish Church by a licence at my own expense. I am endeavouring to obtain a further endowment of £10 a year in mortmain [i.e. from land or property given in perpetuity].

On his death in 1747, in a final piece of generosity, Dr Thomlinson left the school and a house for the master, together with the income from the two galleries, some pews in the church and a further sum of £100 in trust for the school.

The school was enlarged in 1825, by which time it was catering for girls as well as boys, the girls being educated upstairs and the boys downstairs. A house was also built by private subscription for the Mistress. The school was enlarged again in 1889 under the auspices of another great rector and benefactor of Whickham, the Revd Henry Byne Carr, and a stone commemorating the occasion was inserted in the south wall reading:

> Charity Schools
> built and endowed by
> the Revd Dr Thomlinson, Rector
> of this Parish and Prebendary
> of St Paul's London 1742.
> Altered and added to
> by subscriptions.
> The Revd H.B. Carr, MA Rector
> AD 1889.

John Johnston ('Jacky') Robinson

In the eighteenth century and for most of the nineteenth century, the Master of the Parochial school, and later on the Mistress and their staff, were unqualified. Indeed, in the early years, the position of Master was generally a part-time job for the curate. It should be remembered, of course, that the curriculum was very limited being restricted to little more than the 'three Rs'. Despite the lack of qualifications, the most famous, and possibly the most effective, Master belongs to this era.

John Johnston Robinson, universally known as 'Jacky' Robinson, became Master in 1838, and over the next thirty years, until he retired in 1868, created a formidable reputation for the school, with many pupils travelling considerable distances from surrounding villages to attend. Although technically 'unqualified' he had many personal qualifications for the job. In academic terms, he was an excellent arithmetician and penman, but he was also a strong disciplinarian, an essential quality for a sole teacher teaching a school containing as many as 100 boys aged from five to fourteen. It is said that the part of the church occupied by him and his pupils was always the quietest part. He was also very hard-working, acting as post-master as well as school-master, teaching arithmetic at a local boarding school at lunch-time and surveying land for local farmers. Above all, he was a character with a keen sense of humour about whom many stories were told.

A contemporary drawing of 'Jacky' Robinson.

An early (1716) regulation of Charity schools stated that 'a boy must be sent to school clean, washed and comb'd'. Jacky enforced this by sending any boy who arrived with his hair uncombed out into the yard to have his hair brushed with the broom. In another novel use of the implements to hand, he would form an impromptu orchestra from those boys he considered were not singing the morning hymn with sufficient enthusiasm, and have one boy using the poker and coal-rake as a fiddle and bow, another one using the tongs as cymbals and a third using the coal-scuttle and a stick as a drum. Boys who persisted in making an unacceptable amount of noise had a pair of horns fastened to their heads and had to march back and forwards in the school bellowing as much like a bullock as they could manage. Other boys who failed to answer questions satisfactorily would be obliged to wear a dunce's cap or sent to ask the answer from 'Benny Arkless' cuddy' which was usually to be found grazing on the village green.

The village green in use as a school playground, c. 1909.

While it was these stories which established Jacky's reputation as a hard, albeit entertaining, taskmaster, virtue was also rewarded when appropriate, with apples or pennies being handed to successful pupils. Be that as it may, Jacky's presence anywhere in the village was sufficient to command respect even among those who did not attend the school.

As already mentioned, the range of subjects taught at this time was still very limited – the 'three Rs' (Reading, Writing and Arithmetic) with Grammar and Geography – but reading included the Bible and English history so that the range of subjects tended to be a little wider in practice. Reading presented particular problems at a time when many parents were themselves illiterate, and their homes would lack any sort of reading matter never mind reference works like dictionaries and atlases. Much 'homework' in consequence involved seeking out the meanings of words. In addition, the older boys had to write a letter on any topic they wished each weekend for marking and discussion on Monday morning. These were usually about local events so the Master was always kept well-informed about village matters. The school opened and closed with a hymn and a prayer, and Master and pupils attended church every Friday. Jacky died in 1874 at the age of seventy-four and was buried in the churchyard after a funeral service conducted by the Rector, the Revd Henry Byne Carr.

Other Schools

Other small private schools were occasionally opened in the area. Crowley's Swalwell school has already been mentioned. In Whickham, another small school offering boarding facilities for

The Knowles in the nineteenth century when the post office was on the right. The youngsters lurking round the corner may have been trying to avoid the keen eye of 'Jacky' Robinson in the school at the top.

boys was opened in Beech House by a Mr Brown in about 1815. This was subsequently taken over by a Miss Phoebe Simons and turned into a girls boarding school. Another church school was opened in Dunston in 1818 and a number of small 'dame' schools were opened in Whickham itself from time to time. Nothing, however, seems to have challenged the pre-eminence of the Parochial school until the later years of the nineteenth century.

In 1870, the Elementary Education Act was passed and a School Board comprising seven prominent local people was formed. This led to the opening of Swalwell Board school in 1875, and other Board schools followed. In addition, Roman Catholic schools attached to Sacred Heart church at Byermoor and St Philip Neri church in Dunston opened in the 1880s. Despite these developments, pressure on places in the Parochial school continued to increase until the early twentieth century when a number of other new schools, including what is now Whickham Front Street school, were built in the area to cope with the increasing population and the raising of the school leaving age to fourteen years. Finally, in 1972, a replacement building for the Parochial school was built elsewhere in Whickham, but the old school building is still in use to accommodate out-housed council services. In the same year, another Roman Catholic school was built in Whickham itself following the establishment of the Roman Catholic Church of St Mary's.

The hall in Dunston School, 1908. The bearded man was Charles McIntyre, the head teacher.

A class at Dunston School, 1908.

The council has continued to build new and replacement primary schools in the area to cope with the considerable growth in population after the Second World War. There are now, in addition to the Parochial school and three Roman Catholic schools, eight primary schools in the area – four in Whickham itself (Clover Hill, Fellside, Front Street and Washingwell), two in Dunston (Dunston Hill and Riverside) and one each in Marley Hill and Swalwell. There are also two comprehensive schools – Whickham and Kingsmeadow (Dunston).

CHAPTER 10

Some Notable People

Many of the people who have made significant contributions to the history of Whickham have already been mentioned in earlier chapters of this book. In some cases it has seemed appropriate to give fairly full accounts of their achievements as part of the narrative, notably Sir Ambrose Crowley and 'Jacky' Robinson whose stories are inseparable from those of Swalwell and the Parochial school respectively, but others deserve a fuller account of their lives than has been given previously. This chapter is intended to remedy that shortfall and to mention one or two other people who appear here for the first time.

William Shield

William Shield is probably the most famous person to have been born in Swalwell. He was born on 5 March 1748. His father (also William Shield) was a music teacher in the village and young William inherited his father's interest in music, beginning to play the violin at the age of six and the harpsichord some time later.

William Shield Senior died when his son was only nine, leaving behind a widow with four children to raise, and a few years later young William was faced with the problem of learning a trade, being offered a choice between becoming a barber, a sailor or a boat-builder. He chose the latter, which meant that he had to live in South Shields, but he took his violin and his music with him. Fortunately for him, his employer, Edward Davison, encouraged his interest in music and helped him to earn money by playing professionally at concerts.

After completing his boat-building apprenticeship, Shield embarked on a career as a composer, achieving such success that he was appointed Musician in Ordinary to His Majesty George III and was engaged as composer at Covent Garden Theatre. In addition to composing, he wrote text-books on music and at one stage studied painting under the guidance of More, the landscape painter. In 1817, he was appointed 'Master of the Musicians in Ordinary' by King George III.

Shield died on 25 January 1829 and was buried in Westminster Abbey. His music is little known today, although at the time of

William Shield, the composer, 1748-1829.

his death it was very highly regarded. One review claimed that 'After Purcell, we consider Shield to be the finest and most perfect example of really English writers'. One of his operas, *Rosina*, is set in the scenery of Gibside and Winlaton Mill which gives it a particular local interest, but his best-known music today is probably the tune to *Auld Lang Syne*.

Little is known of Shield's private life. He visited Swalwell in 1791 but his visit seems to have aroused little local interest. Both his parents and his sister Ann (who married John Arkless of Whickham) are buried in Whickham churchyard where there is also a commemorative stone to William himself.

Charlton Nesbitt

Charlton Nesbitt, the artist, was born in Swalwell on 24 September 1775. His father, Ralph Nesbitt, was a keelman who, realising that his son was artistically gifted, apprenticed him at the age of fourteen to Thomas Bewick, the wood engraver, in Newcastle. Under Bewick's guidance he sketched and engraved a large number of book illustrations.

In 1799, Nesbitt removed to London, where the quality of his work was recognized by the award of a silver medal from the Society of Arts in 1802, but he disliked life in the capital and returned to Swalwell in 1818. He lived for a number of years in Middletown (on Whickham Bank between Whickham and Swalwell) and maintained a workshop on Market Lane, Swalwell. In addition to his activities as a wood engraver, he was a keen gardener and naturalist, and enjoyed country sports which apparently brought him into conflict with local gamekeepers from time to time.

His mother died on 14 December 1828, at the age of ninety, and two years later he returned to London where he died on 11 November 1838. Possibly, the best known of Nesbitt's work during this time was to provide the illustrations for Gilbert White's *History and Antiquities of Selborne*. While Bewick was an incomparable wood engraver, Nesbitt was certainly the best of his pupils.

Charles Attwood – A Whickham Radical

In the eighteenth and early nineteenth centuries, popular support for parliamentary reform and the extension of civil liberties was widespread. In the 1820s, this movement became a mass movement known as radicalism, its main objects being manhood suffrage and annual parliaments. One of the best-

Charles Attwood, radical reformer, 1791-1875.

known radicals in the north-east was Charles Attwood of Whickham Park.

Charles Attwood was actually born in Shropshire in 1791, but he moved to the north-east in 1810 and spent the rest of his life in the region. He was a businessman who became involved a wide range of business activities. Initially, he set up business as a glass manufacturer on the South Shore in Gateshead, and later added a sawmill and a soda factory, but these do not appear to have been particularly successful. He also bred race-horses but with an equal lack of success. Later on, he became interested in iron-making, at which he proved to be much more successful, acquiring a lease of the ironstone underlying the manors of Wolsingham and Stanhope and building blast furnaces at Tow Law. In around 1825, he moved into Whickham Park from where he took an active interest in the old Mechanics Institute, delivering several lectures on its behalf.

However, it was Attwood's involvement in the movement to obtain political reform which made him famous as one of the foremost platform speakers of his time. Sometime in the late 1820s, he became the joint secretary of the Northern Political Union, a body set up to campaign for parliamentary reform and modelled upon the Birmingham Political Union, a body with similar objectives set up by another member of his family.

In December 1830, Attwood chaired a meeting in Gateshead which resulted in a petition being sent to London seeking parliamentary representation for Gateshead, and by March 1831 he had been chosen by the Northern Political Union to be the

candidate should Gateshead be allocated a member. In May, however, he withdrew his name, preferring to run for Newcastle.

On 7 October 1831, the House of Lords rejected the Whig Government's Reform Bill, which had been bitterly opposed by the Tories, and a mass meeting of protest was held on Newcastle Town Moor. On the morning of the mass meeting, hundreds of workmen from Whickham, Swalwell, Blaydon and Winlaton assembled outside Whickham Park, unharnessed Attwood's horses, and themselves pulled his carriage from Whickham to the Town Moor, with many more of his supporters cheering him along the way.

Later in October, a County demonstration was due to be held in Durham under the chairmanship of another leading radical, Charles John Clavering of Axwell Park, and it was rumoured the Marquis of Londonderry, an opponent of reform was planning to send some of his pitmen to break up the meeting. On this occasion, Crowley's Crew, led by 'Lang Jack' and armed with oak saplings or 'peel grains', marched to the meeting place and surrounded the platform. When the pitmen tried to break up the meeting, Attwood shouted for Crowley's Crew who quickly drove the pitmen from the field and the meeting proceeded without further interruption.

In May 1832, Charles Larkin, in the course of a meeting at the Spital, reminded King William IV of the fate of Louis XVI, and warned Queen Adelaide that 'a fairer head than hers had rolled upon the scaffold' (Attwood dissociated himself from these remarks). Despite his longstanding opposition to electoral reform, King William was eventually prevailed upon to agree to create sufficient peers to ensure the passage of the bill should this prove necessary and, despite some last minute vacillation on his part, the bill eventually became the Reform Act of 1832. Although this Act went only a small part of the way towards meeting the radicals' demands, it did extend the franchise to the upper middle classes, got rid of the rotten and pocket boroughs and gave seats to industrial towns, including Gateshead.

Gateshead's claim to a parliamentary seat was not unopposed. Several other towns had equally strong claims and Gateshead's case had to be argued out in committees of both Houses of Parliament, with spokesmen for Gateshead being briefed by representatives of the Northern Political Union. Debates were lively if not always well informed. One opponent of Gateshead appeared to believe that Newcastle and North Shields were in County Durham, another that Gateshead was merely a suburb of Newcastle. Despite these levels of ignorance, Gateshead finally won the battle for representation, at least partly, it must be said, because of its commitment to the Whig cause and the reform movement.

In the 1832 election which followed, the voting in Newcastle was: Sir M.W. Ridley (the sitting member) 2105, Mr Hodgson 1678, and Charles Attwood 1092. Ironically, the Northern Political Union candidate in Gateshead – Cuthbert Rippon – was elected unopposed. In Birmingham, Thomas Attwood was also elected.

Attwood's supporters, and particularly Crowley's Crew, were bitterly disappointed at his defeat. The Methodists, who had not supported Attwood, produced a pamphlet explaining their reasons and Crowley's Crew collected as many of these pamphlets as they could and burnt them near the Swalwell Methodist Chapel during the Sunday morning service.

Despite his lack of electoral success, Charled Attwood continued throughout the 1830s to campaign for universal suffrage (a target which was only finally achieved in the twentieth century). The radical movement itself was largely absorbed into Chartism following the publication of the People's Charter in 1838, and the presentation of a Charter petition to Parliament by Thomas Attwood in 1839. In that year, Charled Attwood left Whickham and settled in Wolsingham in order to concentrate on his business interests in Weardale. In 1840, he also severed his links with the Gateshead area by selling his Gateshead business to Allhusen's, from where it subsequently passed into the hands of the United Alkali Company which eventually became part of ICI.

Attwood's activities in the Gateshead area occupied a period of thirty years of which only half were spent in Whickham. Nevertheless, his influence was immense. It was through the efforts of Attwood and his colleagues that Gateshead acquired representation in the House of Commons and, if it had not been for what seems to have been an unfortunate error of judgement on his part, he would probably have been Gateshead's first MP.

In Whickham, he seems to have been well-liked, and was respected for his ability, energy and generosity. He died at his home in Wolsingham in 1875 at the age of eighty-five.

The Taylors of Swalwell and Whickham

The Taylor family first appeared in the Whickham parish registers in the sixteenth century as residents of Swalwell, and by the middle of the eighteenth century they were prosperous business people owning a number of wherries used to supply ships with coal and other goods. In 1747, Matthew and John Taylor are recorded as

*The Hermitage,
Whickham, built by
Matthew Taylor in 1790.*

having paid £2 to the Manorial Court for their Wherry Landing at Swalwell. The Taylors most successful venture, however, began in 1765 when they built Swalwell Brewery which became the most important brewing business in the county. The brewery is long since gone, but is still remembered in the name of Brewery Bank on which it was situated opposite the present Swalwell Social Club.

The records of the brewery's customers include the names of many prominent people, including, for example, both the Earl of

The Grange, built by William Taylor in 1823.

Strathmore and Stoney Bowes (the first and second husbands of Mary Eleanor Bowes), the Rectors of both Whickham and Ryton, Sir Thomas Clavering and other members of both the peerage and the local gentry, testifying to the quality of their products.

In 1803, when Napoleon was threatening to invade England, the family's reputation was such that John Taylor was appointed Superintendent of Swalwell with a duty to obtain 'pioneers' to resist the invasion – an early form of 'Dad's Army'. There were obvious advantages in having a brewer in charge of these activities. The Earl of Strathmore's account includes an entry: 'Aug. 19th, 1803. To 5 Bar. Ale for Volunteers', the volunteers in this case apparently consisting of a mounted troop of Gibside cavalry.

In 1790, Matthew Taylor built the Hermitage in Whickham Front Street, which remained in the family until the death of Henry Taylor in 1910. It was subsequently put to a variety of uses, including serving for a time as the village library, and is now used by the council as sheltered housing. The estate was originally landscaped with a look-out tower, tennis court and boating lake. The lake was apparently created on the site of what was known as Prudhoe's Pond and laid out with a pagoda to imitate the traditional Willow Pattern design.

In 1823, the Taylors finally ended their connection with Swalwell when one of their sons, William, built 'The Grange' in Whickham. This is another of Whickham's old houses which no longer exists but its name is recalled in the Grange estate, one of the large areas of modern housing built in Whickham since the end of the Second World War.

The Barras Family

As mentioned in Chapter 2, an early problem which coal-owners had to face was the high cost of wayleaves which were levied by the land-owners to allow coal to be transported across their land. Many farming families made considerable fortunes from wayleaves, the Barras family of yeoman farmers being perhaps the best-known case in Whickham.

In the seventeenth century, the land to the south of the village was covered with coal-pits which sent their coal in wains down Whaggs Lane and Coalway Lane to the staiths at Swalwell and Derwenthaugh. This route took them through the land farmed by the Barras family and by the early eighteenth century, the family had become wealthy on account of the money derived from wayleaves.

John Barras and his wife Isabel both died within a few days of each other in 1724 and are buried in the chancel of Whickham parish church. Their son John married a lady called Frances whose surname is unknown (their marriage is not recorded in the Whickham register) and they built a new house at the Whaggs in the 1740s. The younger John seems to have died shortly after this house was completed and his wife became a very wealthy widow. It was not long, however, before she remarried, this time to the Rector of Whickham. The wedding was reported in the *Newcastle Journal* of 13 October 1750 in the following terms:

> On Monday last, the Revd Dr Williamson of Whickham, in the Co. of Durham, was married at Lamesley to Mrs Barras, a widow gentlewoman of the same place, an agreeable and accomplished lady with a fortune above £10,000.

On her remarriage, the new Mrs Williamson moved into what was then the fairly new Rectory (completed in 1713) and the new house at the Whaggs was offered for sale in the *Journal* of 14 June 1751 as follows:

> To lett against Lady Day next, a new built house of hewn stone, well sashed and pleasantly situated at Whickham, wherein Mrs Barras lately dwelt, consisting of nine fine rooms and good well-ceiled garrats [sic] above them, and large arched cellars below, a back kitchen, brew-house, a very good stable and coach-house, granary and pigeon house well-stocked, with several other conveniences, together with a handsome garden and summer-house, a variety of good wall-fruit and other fruit trees newly planted, and also with or without two fields adjoining for pasture or meadow.

This attractive-sounding residence sadly no longer exists. Mrs Williamson herself died in 1761. Other members of the family also lived in Whickham, notably John Barras, who was a churchwarden for a time and is best remembered for a bitter dispute with another Rector, Dr Thomlinson, about the family pew, but by the end of the eighteenth century the Barras family had all left Whickham.

The Hawks Family

The first Hawks to appear in the Whickham parish registers was William Hawks whose son, Joseph, was baptized on 24 February 1718, to be followed over the years by other children, most of whom were also baptized at Whickham. William was a blacksmith who had apparently come to Swalwell to work at Crowley's Iron Works. He lived for a time in Quality Row, Swalwell, and eventually became a foreman at Crowley's. One of his children, also called William, was born in 1730 but for some reason was not baptized at Whickham although he did complete his apprenticeship as a blacksmith at Crowley's.

In 1749, the elder William moved to Gateshead and set up his own forge which seems to have made the same sort of ironware as that made by Crowley. He died in 1755 and was buried in Gateshead churchyard. After his death, his son William took over the firm and began to expand the business wherever suitable water-power was available to drive the machinery. He erected a rolling-mill and forges at Beamish, a forge at Lumley and acquired works at Bedlington. Increasingly, he was in competition with Crowley's and a machine which enabled chain to be made more efficiently enabled him to win Government contracts which had been held by Crowley's for a century. As Hawk's prospered, Crowley's declined and employees began to move from Swalwell and Winlaton to Gateshead.

When the younger William died in 1810, his eldest son Robert Shafto Hawks became head of the firm and was followed in turn by his nephew, George, who became the first Mayor of Gateshead in 1835. By 1863 the firm was employing 1,500 workers, far more than the 1,000 which Crowley's had employed at their peak. Although the firm was based in Gateshead, other members of the family continued to live in the Whickham area, and one descendant, Jane Hawks, was married in Whickham on 2 August, 1807 to Robert Clasper of Dunston, their issue including Harry Clasper, the famous Tyneside oarsman.

Harry Clasper, the great oarsman, 1812-1870, in action.

Harry Clasper

Harry was actually born in Dunston in 1812 and began his working life as a pitman but while still in his teens he became a wherryman on the Tyne, and thereafter soon acquired a reputation as an oarsman at a time when rowing was as big a spectator sport as soccer is today and races took place on the Tyne between the old Tyne Bridge and Lemington Point. In addition to racing on the Tyne, on which he was accepted as the champion, he competed in many other parts of the country including the Thames, Mersey, Clyde, Loch Lomond and elsewhere. In 1845, he won the world team championship in partnership with two brothers and an uncle, and became Scottish solo champion on two occasions in the 1850s. When Harry began rowing, the boats used in competition were the same boats which served at other times as pleasure boats or were used to carry goods and passengers. In consequence, they tended to be both wide and heavy to row. Harry's greatest achievement, which reinforced his record as an outstanding sportsman, was probably the invention of a boat designed purely for competition – the outrigger racing scull, which was both light and slim and has served as the model for the boats used in competitive rowing ever since. A song of the time ran:

> Ov a' yor grand rowers iv skiff or iv skull,
> There's nyne wi' wor Harry hes chance for to pull;
> Man, he sits like a duke an' he fethers se free, Oh!
> Harry's the lad, Harry Clasper for me!

Haud away, Harry! Canny lad, Harry.
Harry's the king of the Tyems an' the Tyne.

Harry smothers them a' for he beels his awn boat;
But nyen like hissel', man, can set her afloat.
He cuts through the Tyne like a fish i' the sea,
An' the lasses a' shoot, as he shuts by the Key.

Haud away, Harry! Canny lad, Harry.
Harry's the king of the Tyems an' the Tyne.

In the 1860s, he gave up competitive rowing and concentrated increasingly on boat-building and training younger aspirants but his sporting achievements were celebrated with a testimonial which raised enough money to buy him a house in Scotswood Road, Newcastle where he traded as a licensed victualler. The festivities included a dinner at Balmbra's Music Hall on 5 June 1862 at which Geordie Ridley, the well-known local singer and song-writer, sang a new song, *The Blaydon Races*, which has since become the 'Geordie National Anthem'. Harry died at Newcastle-upon-Tyne in 1870 and his funeral was a massive affair. His remains were carried through Newcastle and then taken up-river on a wherry as far as Derwenthaugh, from where a procession led by a brass band proceeded to Whickham churchyard. The roads, bridges and river-banks were crowded with spectators and in all it is estimated that 130,000 people attended to pay their last respects to a local folk hero. The *Annals of Whickham* record that 'the number of people attending the funeral was probably the largest ever seen at Whickham.'

The inscription on the memorial to Harry Clasper in Whickham churchyard was written by a former Rector of Whickham, Revd Henry B. Carr, and reads:

Beneath this monument, reared to his memory, by the ardent affection of friends and admirers from every class, and from all parts of the kingdom, and in this sacred spot commanding a full view of that noble river, the well-beloved scene of former triumphs, rest the mortal remains of Henry (Harry) Clasper, the accomplished oarsman and boat builder of Derwenthaugh who died July 12th, 1870, aged 58 years. 'Know ye not that they which run in a race run all, but one receiveth the prize. So run that ye may obtain.' I. Cor. ix.24.'

The memorial to Harry Clasper in Whickham churchyard.

After Harry's death, his two sons, John and Harry, set up a boathouse in Putney where they built racing boats for clubs all over the world including those of both Cambridge and Oxford Universities.

There is another Clasper memorial in the churchyard which is worthy of note. Immediately behind the memorial to Harry is one formed like the prow of a skiff which was erected in 1849 by Harry and his brothers to the memory of their parents, Robert and Jane, and two of their brothers, Edward and John, who had died tragically early. Jane died in 1832 when she was only forty-six and Robert in 1841 aged fifty-seven. Edward was twenty-five when he died in 1845 and John was drowned in the Tyne in 1847 while preparing for a race when he was only twenty.

Thomas 'Tommy' Heron ('Skipper')

In the main, voluntary organizations are run by unpaid volunteers who generally, as the saying goes, 'receive more in the way of kicks than ha'pence.' There are many such people in Whickham, as no doubt there are elsewhere, but one volunteer may serve as a representative of them all.

The 1st Whickham (St Mary's) Scout Group was founded in 1915 with a Mr Thompson as Scout Master. Mr Thompson died suddenly in 1916 and Tommy Heron somewhat unexpectedly became Scout Master in his place, thereby beginning what became sixty years of service to the Scout movement. Under Tommy's leadership, and despite his absence for a time on war service, the group grew rapidly, reaching three active sections (Cubs, Scouts and Rovers) by 1922 and erecting new headquarters in a field north of the church in 1929. In 1939, Tommy was awarded the

Medal of Merit for service to scouting, which was followed by the Silver Acorn (one of Scouting's highest honours) in 1955. He finally retired in 1976 at the age of seventy-eight, and sadly died in the following year leaving, it is estimated, around 3,000 boys and men he had helped and influenced over the years.

In addition to his work for the Scout movement, Tommy Heron was also sexton and a churchwarden of St Mary's for many years, so his contribution to the life of the community made him very much an institution in the village.

The memorial to Harry Clasper's parents and brothers in Whickham churchyard.

CHAPTER 11

Local Government

Middle Ages

Somewhere, local government is defined as 'that part of the government of a nation or state which deals mainly with such matters as concern the inhabitants of a particular district or place, and which it is thought desirable should be administered by a Local Authority subordinate to the central government', and it would obviously be inappropriate to finish this history of Whickham without some reference to its local government. In the Middle Ages, when Whickham was still a simple farming community and tiny in comparison with modern Whickham, it was governed by the Bishop of Durham through one of his Halmote Courts and his local agent, the reeve. As coal-mining, and later other industries, developed and the population grew, so life became more complex at the same time as the powers of the Bishop were declining. Some form of local administration was needed to fill the resultant gap.

Initially, the existing parish authorities assumed an increased importance. As mentioned earlier, the churchwardens and leading citizens, usually the more affluent members of local society, became in most areas a sort of self-appointed local authority, co-opting members as necessary up to some pre-determined number. A formal title might be 'select vestry' or some similar expression, but the body was usually known as the 'four-and-twenty' and this was the name by which they were known in Whickham.

Although, to modern eyes, this situation was still most undemocratic, it did at least replace rule by a relatively remote authority, the Bishop of Durham, with rule by a group of local people. In any case, at that time democracy itself was regarded by many, if not most, people as a revolutionary, completely unacceptable idea (witness the burning of an effigy of Thomas Paine in Swalwell in 1793), and ordinary people were also much more deferential to those they regarded as 'their betters'. The situation was formalised in the Poor Relief Act of 1601, which required the appointment of Overseers of the Poor who were to be the churchwardens together with 'substantial householders' – in other words the 'four-and-twenty'. The Poor Relief Act was of long-term significance for two reasons. First, the Overseers of the Poor had a very long life as a corporate body, remaining in existence for over 300 years until 1925; although from 1834, under the Poor Law Amendment Act, they were responsible only for valuations and rate collection, the responsibility for poor relief being transferred to Boards of Guardians. Second, and more importantly, the Act created the power to levy rates, albeit only to support the poor of the parish at first.

The Beginnings of Modern Local Government

Modern local government did not begin to emerge until much later, in the early nineteenth century, when a number of Acts were passed authorizing the creation of Local Boards of Health, and the levying of rates to pay for the police and for road lighting and maintenance. However, it was not until 1875 that Whickham acquired a Board of Health and gas-lit roads.

This piecemeal approach to local government was replaced by a more comprehensive one in the later years of the nineteenth century when Acts between 1875 and 1890 led, *inter alia*, to the creation of Durham County Council and Whickham Urban District Council, each with its own specified duties and powers. Whickham's first representative on Durham County Council was Lord Ravensworth, suggesting that the habits of deference were still strong. Whickham's first Council of twelve members was elected in 1894 and took over the functions of the Whickham Board of Health, although, as already indicated, the Board of Guardians and the Overseers of the Poor continued well into the twentieth century.

Whickham council offices when Whickham Urban District Council still existed (note the inscription on the notice board).

Throughout the twentieth century, the population of the area increased enormously and a large number of Acts placed increasingly onerous duties and powers upon the local authorities. By the beginning of the 1970s, Durham County Council was responsible for education, police, fire service, main roads and bridges, libraries and a variety of health services, while Whickham UDC was responsible for a range of other services including sewerage, refuse collection, housing, parks, local roads. cemeteries and public lighting.

At this time, Whickham Council comprised twenty members representing five wards based roughly upon the traditional four 'quarters', with Whickham, because of its growth in population, being split into two. Dunston elected eight members, Whickham East three, Whickham West three, Swalwell three and Marley Hill (including Sunniside) three. The area also elected two members to Durham County Council, one from Dunston and the other from the remaining three wards.

Re-organization in the Early 1970s
The national government carried out a major restructuring of local government. Locally, this led to Whickham UDC and a number of other local authorities on the south bank of the Tyne (Gateshead, Felling, Blaydon, Ryton and Birtley) being brought together into a new Gateshead Metropolitan Borough Council. At the same time, Gateshead MBC, together with the other new-style borough councils of Newcastle, Sunderland, North Tyneside and South Tyneside, were also joined together in a completely new County Council called Tyne and Wear, but this, along with other new-style county councils, was abolished some years later. The new Gateshead MBC originally had seventy-eight members, although this was later reduced to sixty-six, with Whickham's overall representation being reduced to nine – three from Dunston, three from Whickham North (comprising Swalwell and Whickham East), and three from Whickham South (comprising Whickham West and MarleyHill/ Sunniside). Until Tyne and Wear County Council was abolished, Whickham was also represented by three county councillors – one from each of the new wards.

In recent years, national governments have reversed previous trends and have followed policies designed to reduce the scope of local government, with powers being transferred to national government or to quangos of various sorts, and council finances being subjected to extremely tight control. Despite this, the range of services for which local councils are responsible remains extremely large and Gateshead Council's budget for the present year (2001-2002) amounts to over £200 million, nearly half of which is for education. Other services include leisure activities, libraries, arts and information, social services, housing, community safety, economic development, highways and construction, commercial and consumer services, planning, design, cleansing and waste disposal, with separate levies to cover passenger transport, the probation service, environment agency, Port Health Authority, police and fire services. As this list indicates, in many ways the local council still has a greater impact on people's lives than the central government itself, yet fewer people vote in local elections than in national elections.

Despite severe cutbacks in spending and other restrictions in recent years, local government remains very big business indeed compared with the days of the four-and-twenty, and it is difficult to visualise how many of the services provided could be organized in any other way without loss of democratic control. Debate on the future structure of local government still continues, however, with some form of decentralized (parish?) council for Whickham still remaining a possibility.

Walking Tour

WALKING TOUR

Although there are many interesting buildings to be seen in other parts of the Whickham area, this walk covers only the historic centre of Whickham, most of which is a conservation area containing a large number of listed buildings and reflecting its initial development as a linear village along Front Street. Photographs of the area as it is today are contained in the earlier colour section. The illustrations in this section show the area as it was in the early years of the twentieth century, mainly around 1900, with some photographs dating from the 1920s.

> **Start walking westwards along Whickham Highway from the top of Dunston Bank, keeping to the footpath on the right-hand side.**

A map of Whickham Highway and the east end of Whickham as they were in 1898.

The estate on the right is Dunston Hill, ancestral home of the Carrs whose many noteworthy contributions to Whickham's history are recorded in the History section. Dunston Hill has served as a hospital for many years but, at the time of writing, the hall itself is boarded up. Further along the Highway, the

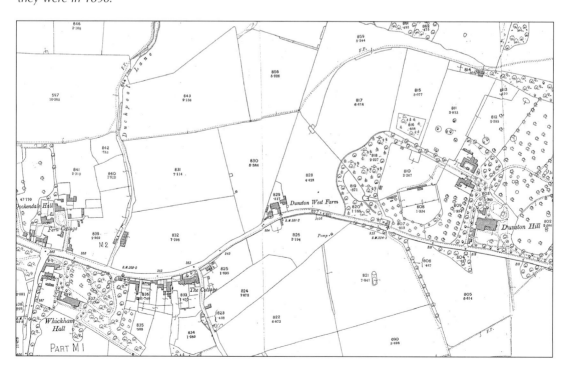

first buildings within the village itself are also on the right and comprise the former Dunston West Farm, now a riding school. In the 'banky fields' behind the farm buildings are the remains of some early (seventeenth- and eighteenth-century) mine-workings and wagonways which have been listed for their historical interest. The Lakes housing estate and Whickham police station are to the west of the farm. The housing estate is so named because the names of almost all the roads are derived from the Lake District including Borrowdale, Bowness, Buttermere, Coniston, Derwentwater, Grasmere and Windermere.

> *At this point you will need to cross the Highway (with great care – there are blind bends in both directions) because the footpath switches sides. If you are interested in early railway history, you may wish to make a short detour up Washingwell Lane on this (south) side of the Highway.*

Washingwell Lane, leading to the former Washingwell Farm and Washingwell Wood, has a very old name and is shown on the oldest available maps, but is apparently derived from a Saxon named *Wassa* rather than a well used for washing. There was a well situated about halfway between the farm and the wood, but there seems to be no trace of it remaining today. A short distance up Washingwell Lane, on the right hand side, the remains of an old wagonway embankment dating from the early eighteenth century can still be seen alongside some allotments. This was probably part of the wagonway which subsequently ran behind Dunston West Farm. Further up Washingwell Lane, just before Washingwell Wood is reached, lies the site of Washingwell Roman fort discovered by Professor Norman McCord of Newcastle University in 1970, but the site has never been excavated and there is nothing visible at ground level.

> *Return to Whickham Highway and continue walking in a westerly direction, keeping to the footpath on the south side of the Highway.*

On this side of the Highway are a number of attractive seventeenth- and eighteenth-century houses which date from the time when coal-mining was moving away from the village and it was becoming

Walking Tour

Walking Tour

Children at the foot of Washingwell Lane, c. 1900, opposite the site of the modern police station.

Looking west from the end of Duckpool Lane, early twentieth century. The Orchard is on the immediate right, with access to Dockendale Lane and the site of the modern filling station further along on the same side. The junction with Broom Lane is ahead on the left.

a fashionable place to live. Among them is Beech House, which was in use as a boys' school in the early nineteenth century. Both the future Lord Armstrong and Henry Byne Carr, a member of the Carr family of Dunston Hill who would become a notable Rector of Whickham, are believed to have been educated here. It later became a girls' school before reverting to its original use as a private residence. Another of these houses is 'Pink House', which at one time was used as a sweet shop, presumably to cater for the pupils at the nearby Beech House.

> **Pause on reaching the neighbourhood of The Orchard on the right-hand side of the road, immediately after the police station.**

At this point, Whickham Highway becomes Front Street, the main road through Whickham itself. On the right hand (north) side are two more very old names – Duckpool Lane and Dockendale Lane – separated by The Orchard. Facing them, on the south side of Front Street, is Whickham Lodge, another elegant mansion now divided into separate dwellings with adjoining modern houses which have been given the name Whickham Lodge Rise. Bourn's late nineteenth-century history of Whickham gives this account of the area:

> One the north side of the park of the Williamsons [i.e. Whickham Lodge] is a road known as the Duckpool, which branches from the turnpike [i.e. Whickham Highway/Front Street], and terminates in a field path to Dunston. Formerly, opposite the entrance of the road was a farmhouse, and at the 'Duck Pool' there was a large pool of water, which was much frequented by the ducks belonging to the farm, which accounts for the name of the place. A little westward, on the north side of the turnpike, is another road, which leads to Dockendale Hall, the residence of Miss Taylor, who belongs to one of the old families of Whickham. The house stands on the margin of the old 'Easter Dayle' and 'Wester Dayle' which formed part of the common lands 200 years ago. Doubtless, the old mansion received its name from the Dayles and the quantity of the Common Docken which grew in the neighbourhood.

More recently, it has been suggested that the 'Duck Pool' may have served a less comfortable purpose as a ducking pool for offenders. A short distance down Duckpool Lane, on the right hand side, a group of two storey rubble stone cottages, which probably date from the early nineteenth century and may have been wagonmens' cottages, make an interesting contrast to the surrounding twentieth century buildings, although doors, windows and roofs have been extensively modernised.

The small Orchard housing estate is relatively new, dating from the 1960s when it won a design award, but an orchard has occupied the site for many years, possibly centuries, and the apple, pear and plum trees continue to be a target for all the small, and some not so small, children in the neighbourhood every autumn.

Behind The Orchard are other modern roads with names reflecting local people, places and events. Orchard Road, for example, was presumably named after the same orchard before houses were built on the orchard itself. Cromwell Road recalls

Walking Tour

Oliver Cromwell's passage through Whickham with his army when he is reputed to have stayed at Dockendale Hall. Crowley Avenue is named after the Crowley of Crowley's Ironworks whose history was bound up with the development of Swalwell as an industrial centre. Lambton Avenue recalls the Lambton family of 'Lambton Worm' fame.

Just beyond the Orchard, on the corner of Dockendale Lane, is a cottage which may have been the eighteenth century toll house at which tolls were levied upon travellers using the turnpike road running from Gateshead via Lobley Hill, Whickham Highway, Front Street and down Swalwell Bank en route to Hexham. There was certainly a toll house in this area but another school of thought believes that it was situated in a slightly different position and was demolished many years ago. Dockendale Lane leads to Dockendale Hall, which dates from the sixteenth century and is one of the oldest surviving houses in Whickham. Oliver Cromwell is believed to have stayed here when he passed through the area in both 1648 and 1650. This may well have occurred because Cromwell liked to humiliate his enemies by commandeering their homes, and at that time the house belonged to Sir Thomas Liddell of Ravensworth who was a prominent Royalist. After many changes of ownership over the centuries, the estate was purchased in 1947 by the Catholic Church which lacked a physical presence in Whickham. Initially, the hall itself served as the presbytery with the refurbished stables as the church until a new church and presbytery were built and came into use in 1973. The hall has since been sold and is now occupied as four flats, the stables serving yet another purpose as the parish hall. Sadly, the hall is now hidden behind a large modern garage.

On the opposite (south) side of Front Street, Whickham Lodge was once surrounded by nineteen acres of parkland, now largely covered by modern housing. The 'Williamsons' referred to in the quotation above were the family of the Revd William Williamson who came from a well-known Newcastle family called Hopper but changed his name to Williamson as part of a marriage settlement. The house was subsequently bought by Priestman Collieries (owners of Axwell Park Colliery) to house their agent and later belonged to Mr Reed, the proprietor of Venture Coaches.

Move on to the traffic lights adjacent to the garage on the right-hand side of the road.

On the south side of Front Street are the houses known as The

Mews, followed by Broom Lane, which acquired its name from the quantity of broom which used to grow in the area and which is referred to in *The Pitman's Courtship* of 1818: 'An' wor Dick, that leeves ower by High Whickham, He'll myek us broom bussoms for nowse.' The Watergate housing estate on the eastern side of Broom Lane is interesting for a number of reasons, including the name of the estate itself, which originated about a mile away, and the origins of many of the road names.

In the early 1920s, Priestman Collieries sank two shafts in Watergate Wood to form the Watergate Colliery, but built houses for their workers some distance away at this site in Whickham. What was originally the Watergate housing estate quickly became just 'Watergate'. At the time that Priestmans began their Watergate estate, Broadpool Cottage still stood near the site of the pond known as the Broad Pool alongside Broom Lane, and the South Field and Buck's Hill lay further south. The company preserved the name of the Broad Pool in Broadpool Green and Broadpool Terrace, while the South Field gave its name to Southfield Gardens, Southfield Green, Southfield Road and Southfield Terrace. Buck's Hill gave rise to Buck's Hill View, and Broom Lane itself fathered Broom Green, Broom Terrace and Broom Close.

When Whickham Council later enlarged the estate, they named several roads after well-known socialist personalities. Two remain – Lansbury Road, named after George Lansbury, one-time leader of the Labour Party, and Arthur Cook Avenue, in honour of the famous miners' leader. Two others, however, – Lenin Drive and Marx Crescent-are now just The Drive and The Crescent.

On the other (western) side of Broom Lane, lie Cornmoor Road and Cornmoor Gardens which recall the Corn Moor across which these roads were built, and Millfield Road and Millfield Court which similarly recall the Mill Field adjoining the mill of which the remains still stand in Whickham Chase Park. Tethercock Farm occupied much of this area, and when the small estate now called 'The Court' was built a few years ago, it was originally proposed to call it Tethercock Court, but residents objected to the link with blood sports so the name was changed.

At the foot of Broom Lane is the main entrance to Whickham Chase Park which stretches for about 300 yards along the south side of Front Street. Its attractions have helped Whickham to win Britain in Bloom awards on many occasions but are concealed from the casual passerby because the park rises away from road level and is protected by a high stone wall and a belt of trees. The

Walking Tour

The foot of Broom Lane showing the group of houses known as 'The Mews'.

THE MEWS, WHICKHAM.

park originally comprised the grounds of another of Whickham's great mansions, Whickham House, which dated from the early eighteenth century. It was originally the property of the Leaton family but changed hands several times until it was acquired by a mineral water manufacturer called Wilkinson who sold it to the council in 1937. The house itself was used for Civil Defence purposes during the Second World War but was finally demolished in 1960. The remains of the old mill which gave Millfield Road its name stand in the south part of the park. It is not known when it was built nor when it ceased operating. The date of 1567 carved over its doorway is almost certainly incorrect as the style of carving is inconsistent with the date. It is generally believed that whatever date (if any) originally existed was 'improved' when the building was being tidied up at some stage. 1567 was, in fact, the year in which the *Annals of Whickham* record that 'the tenants of Whickham were ordered before the next court to pay for the carrying of millstones or forfeit xls (forty shillings or two pounds)', but a mill probably existed on the site long before this date. It was certainly still working well into the nineteenth century.

> **Use the pedestrian crossing facility to cross to the right-hand (north) side of Front Street.**

Another group of two-storey rubble stone cottages with pantile roofs stand on the north side of Front Street facing the foot of Broom Lane and adjoining the garage mentioned earlier. These probably date from the late eighteenth century and hence are

slightly older than those in Duckpool Lane, but despite this have been subject to fewer structural alterations. It is outside these cottages that Wesley is believed to have preached when he visited Whickham in 1752.

Continue in a westerly direction.

A short distance past the stone cottages lies the entrance to Whickham Park (not to be confused with Whickham Chase Park), which was occupied at various times by several local dignitaries, including the nineteenth century reformer Charles Attwood. This has been converted into flats with a small housing estate in the grounds.

Further along, past the Bay Horse, one of Whickham's oldest pubs, is the lane known as The Knowles, leading to School Lane.

Turn right up The Knowles towards School Lane.

School Lane derives its name from the Parochial School which served the community from 1742 until a replacement was built in 1972 although the old building is still in use to provide local services by Gateshead Council. In the past 'Knowles' appears to have been spelt as *Knole* or *Nowels* and it seems probable that the name is really derived from the knoll or small rise on which the school stands. Whickham's first post office was located here from some time before 1850 at the west end of the Bay Horse, but has subsequently occupied a series of different locations around the village. A dwelling called Postman's Cottage still stands in School Lane opposite the former Parochial school.

The former council offices of Whickham Urban District Council stand on the western side of The Knowles. Whickham Council was formed in 1880 but the council offices were not brought into use until 1904. As the result of local government reorganization in the early 1970s, Whickham and a number of other local authorities were amalgamated to form Gateshead Metropolitan Borough Council with headquarters in Gateshead itself. Like the Parochial school, however, the council offices continue to provide a number of local council services. The main structure has remained largely unchanged since it was built, apart from the recent provision of a ramp to improve access, but the grounds have seen many alterations including the removal of the original high surrounding

Walking Tour

Looking east from near the Bay Horse, showing the entrance to Whickham Park on the left and the wall of Whickham Chase Park on the right.

The Bay Horse before extensive modifications took place in the second half of the twentieth century.

wall and the addition of a war memorial commemorating the dead of two world wars. Behind the council offices is Park Cottage, which carries a date of 1791, although this is usually obscured by ivy. This attractive building was originally two cottages, for the use of the Whickham Park head gardener and coachman, separated by an arch giving access for coaches.

> **Proceed along School Lane to reach the parish church of St Mary the Virgin, the churchyard and Church Green.**

The church is partly Norman, and while it has been subject to extensive alterations and repairs over the centuries, it still encapsulates much of the history of Whickham. The churchyard contains a number of interesting gravestones, some of them dating

Walking Tour

back as much as four hundred years, which also help to cast light on Whickham's past. The history of the green, on the other hand, is somewhat obscure until the mid-nineteenth century when an attempt by a man named Atkins to take possession of it led to the then Rector, Revd H.B. Carr, persuading his brother, Ralph Carr-Ellison, to buy it for the community. It is now maintained by the council. (The history of the church and its surroundings are described in more detail in the accompanying history, above.) At the north-east corner of the green, a building which currently serves as a baker's shop was formerly a coach house for the locally well-known Clavering family for use during their attendance at church services. A house on the west side of the green was once the home of the Atkins who claimed possession of the green but by 1890 had become the second home of the post office which remained there until 1907 when it removed back to a location in the Knowles. Beyond the house is Library Place, so called because a small shop there once housed an equally small lending library.

> **At the north-west corner of the green, take the short footpath known as Dog Loup into Church Chare and then walk west along Church Chare.**

Dog Loup (i.e. Dog Leap) is an interesting name whose origin is now lost in time. It has been suggested that it may refer to dogs being chased out of the adjoining churchyard by the church wardens and 'louping' over the wall, or it may be a comment on the short length of the path ('only a dog loup'). Church Chare is the old lane leading to the church and contains a number of

The view eastwards from the village centre in the 1920s. The Rose and Crown Hotel, substantially re-built twice in the second half of the twentieth century and now re-named Ye Olde Lang Jack, is on the immediate left. The parish church and council offices are further along and set back from the road behind the trees visible on the left-hand side.

Walking Tour

very old houses many of which formerly belonged to the church. Immediately opposite the top of Dog Loup is the sixteenth century Rectory, the oldest surviving residence in the village and once known as Whickham Hall. It was used as the Rectory until 1713 when a former Rector found it too small for his needs and moved to a new Rectory on the other side of Front Street. In 1922 the then Rector moved back into the Whickham Hall building which has served as the Rectory ever since.

Further along, on the same side of Church Chare, is the old Coach House, which has served a variety of uses over the years including operating at different times as a garage, dance hall, cinema, bingo hall and even a skating rink. It is now a fitness centre. Immediately beyond the Coach House is the village tea room which was originally a tithe barn. The road to the right is Coalway Lane which many years ago was the road down which coal wains passed on their way to the river. Some older residents refer to Coalway Lane as Coalwell Lane or Coalywell Lane, recalling the Coal Well and Coalwell House which were situated part way down the hill.

Beyond Coalway Lane is Rose Villa, formerly the home of the late Dr Andrew (Andy) Smith, a much loved and respected doctor in Whickham, whose forebears, including another Dr Andrew Smith, lived in the house for over a hundred years.

In front of Rose Villa, Church Chare rejoins Front Street at what is known as The Cross, not for any religious reason but because that was the point at which the coal wains coming through the village crossed Front Street on their way to the river.

The view westwards from the village centre in the 1920s. This site is the Cross where wains used to cross the road en route to the staiths. The former Rose and Crown Hotel is on the right hand side with the access to Church Chare beyond. Rectory Lane, leading to Whaggs Lane, is on the left.

Walking Tour

Rectory Cottage adjoining the entrance to the former Rectory.

Whaggs Lane in the 1920s.

Pause at this point.

The monument here is to the memory of John (Lang Jack) English, a local strong man whose story is recounted in the above history section of this book. The monument used to stand elsewhere in Whickham adjoining the site of Lang Jack's cottage but was re-erected here by Bellway, the building firm, after it was vandalised in its original position. The nearby public house, formerly the Rose and Crown, has been re-named Ye Olde Lang Jack in his honour. On the opposite corner, the building which currently contains a dentist and a bank after a period as a grocer's shop was formerly Cross House Farm.

Walking Tour

Looking west from the Cross, c. 1900. Cross House Farm, now a bank and dentist's surgery is on the right.

A westward view, c. 1900, with the site of the new shopping centre on the right.

On the opposite (south) side of Front Street is Rectory Lane which acquired its name from the building on the right hand side which, as explained above, served as the Rectory from 1713 to 1922. After it ceased to be the Rectory, the building was converted into a cottage hospital by Dr Andy Smith and his family and continued as such until after the Second World War. An attempt to close it in 1979 created a storm of protest during which sufficient money was raised to install a badly needed lift. Sadly, the drive towards large centrally situated hospitals finally led to its closure and conversion into a nursery school in the late 1980s. At the time of writing, a new health centre and sheltered accommodation are being developed on the site. Some few hundred yards further south, Rectory Lane becomes Whaggs Lane which derives its name from the Whaggs, the large mansion or farm of the Barras family to which it once led.

Walking Tour

> **Walk westwards from the Cross, staying on the right-hand side of the road.**

In this area there has been extensive re-development on both sides of Front Street, which has resulted in the loss of many old buildings, although some old properties still remain. West of the grounds of the old rectory, the south side now contains a telephone exchange and a small modern housing estate.

On the north side, immediately to the west of the former Cross House Farm is St Mary's Green, a modern shopping area, and the Gibside Arms Hotel, which were developed during the 1970s and 1980s. While the area was being re-developed, an old butcher's shop on the site, rather than being simply demolished, was taken down piece by piece with a view to re-erecting it at the Beamish Open-Air Museum. The name St Mary's is derived from the parish church and Gibside reflects the local Gibside estate, described in the above history section, which was the ancestral home of the Bowes family, from whom Queen Elizabeth the Queen Mother is descended.

> **Pause in the vicinity of the Gibside Arms Hotel.**

Surrounded on three sides by the Gibside Arms Hotel is the 1871 Spoor Memorial Chapel, the name of which commemorates a remarkable local man, the Revd Joseph Spoor. Joseph Spoor was born in Whickham in 1813 and began work on the keels as a boy, but subsequently became a minister and noted preacher with the Primitive Methodists. The village pinfold once occupied a position in front of the site of the chapel. Beyond the hotel, in Back Row, a self-explanatory name, are Whickham Salerooms which were originally built after the First World War as a Miners' Welfare Hall but have been used for their present purpose since 1966. On the opposite side of Front Street is the Glebe housing estate, built, as the name suggests, on former church land. Prior to the estate being built, the Glebe Farm was situated here until it was demolished in 1960, and part of the stone boundary wall of the farm is still in existence, now incorporating the stones of the old village pump which also once stood here. This pump was the main source of water for the village prior to mains water being brought in in the 1880s, although there were several other wells in the village including the Washing Well and the Coal Well.

Walking Tour

Carry on walking in a westerly direction.

Beyond this point, there are a number of attractive old houses on the south side of Front Street, several of them listed buildings, although some of them still had *netties* (outside toilets) in front of them until quite recently. The first house, at the eastern end of the row with a window built on the corner, was adapted to serve initially as a baker's shop and later as an electrical shop.

On the north side of Front Street, and situated immediately opposite these houses, is the Square, another shopping development, which has housed the present post office since 1988. Beyond the Square, a small group of older houses still remains. These include another of Whickham's old public houses, the former Three Tuns, now renamed the Bridle Path.

Pause outside the Bridle Path.

A short distance down the road to the right is Whickham Front Street school, the first new school to be opened in Whickham (in 1909) when the Parochial school could no longer cope with the increasing population. Opposite to the Bridle Path, on the south side of Front Street, is the Hermitage. This building dates from 1790 and was the home of Mathew Taylor, proprietor of Swalwell Brewery, and his descendants until 1910 when it passed out of the family's hands. Thereafter it continued in use as a private residence for a time, first for a doctor and then for the manager of what became Norwood Coke Works in Team Valley. In the 1920s it became a library and during the depression served for a time as an office for the local relieving officer. Some time after the Second World War, it was converted to its present use as a council residential hostel.

Next to the Hermitage stands the Whickham Community Centre, originally built as offices for the Medical Officer in 1875. Around the end of the nineteenth century it became a recreation centre and was rebuilt in 1910 as a colliery institute offering a wide range of leisure activities including a library and a reading room. It also served as a soup kitchen during the 1921 and 1926 miners' strikes. After Axwell Park Colliery closed in 1953, it was taken over by the Durham County Council and later Gateshead Council to serve its present function.

> **Carry on to the next set of traffic lights.**

Shortly after the Community Centre, Fellside Road branches off to the south. This was at one time the main road southwards and was not merely the road along the fell side but the road leading to the hamlet of Fellside. Although Fellside Road is now flanked by massive housing estates on either side, the names of a number of old roads opening off it recall features of Whickham's past including Burnthouse Lane which is self-explanatory, Grange Lane which once led to Whickham Grange, Hole Lane leading to the depression known as Gellesfield Hole, Clockburn Lane running alongside the Clock Burn down to the River Derwent, and Woodhouse Lane running past a Wood House which has long since disappeared. The ancient estates of Gibside and Hollinside also adjoin Fellside Road.

At this point we have reached the top of Whickham Bank, the road down to Swalwell, which is nearly the end of our walk through Whickham. It is at this end of the village, however, that Whickham's coal-mining history was most clearly in evidence.

Two groups of older terraced houses which are clustered round the top of Whickham Bank recall the old mine-owners' practice of using family Christian names for their property. On the Whickham Bank itself are Edith Terrace and Eleanor Terrace, while George Street, James Street, Thomas Street and William Street lie in the angle between Whickham Bank and Fellside Road. The colliery itself stood a short distance down the bank on the left hand side where Bank Top Hamlet now stands, and the pithead buildings were still in existence until quite recently. These links with Whickham's coal-mining past seem to make an appropriate conclusion to this walk through Whickham.

The view eastwards from near the top of Whickham Bank, c. 1900. The Bridle Path (formerly the Three Tuns) is at the near end of the terrace on the left.

FURTHER PLACES TO VISIT

As indicated at the beginning of this section, the proposed walk covers only the Whickham village centre, and there are many other places in the area worth visiting. Two in particular should not be missed by visitors although both involve admission charges and necessitate the use of a car.

The Gibside estate, an ancestral home of the Queen Mother, is on the Whickham side of the River Derwent near Rowlands Gill about 2 ½ miles south of the centre of Whickham village and is described in the above history section. The estate now belongs to the National Trust and is open daily (except Mondays) throughout the year. There is a shop on the site which provides ample material to guide visitors round the estate as well as offering refreshments and souvenirs.

For anyone interested in the history of railways and old steam engines, the preserved section of the Tanfield Railway (also mentioned in the above history section) is well worth a visit. It is operated by a volunteer Preservation Society, and is situated near Marley Hill on the road to Stanley, about 1 ½ miles south of Whickham. At the time of writing it is open on Sundays throughout the year, plus Bank Holiday Mondays, and Wednesdays and Thursdays in the summer months, and offers short train journeys including a visit to the Causey Arch.

BIBLIOGRAPHY

Anon. *Parish Church of St Mary the Virgin, Whickham*. Published by the church, undated.

Anon. *Presbyterian Church, Swalwell*. Published by the church, 1933.

Anon. *St Nicholas Church, Dunston*. Published by the church, 1965.

Bennett, Carole. *A Walk Around Whickham*. Whickham and District Local History Society, *c.* 1995.

Bourn, William. *Annals of the Parish of Whickham*. Reprinted in *Focus* magazine, published by Whickham U.D.C. 1966-1968.

Bourn, William. *Our Old Families*. 1915.

Bourn, William. *Whickham Parish: Its History, Antiquities and Industries*. G.&T. Coward, The Wordsworth Press, Carlisle, 1893. Reprinted by Gateshead M.B.C., Portcullis Press, 1999.

Brazendale, Alan. *Whickham, Swalwell and Dunston*. Tempus Publishing Limited, Stroud, 1998.

Brazendale, Alan. Various booklets and articles on the histories of Whickham,Swalwell and Dunston. 1990 onwards.

Edwards, R.W. *Whickham Parochial (Controlled) Junior Mixed and Infants' school, 1714-1964*. A.A. Fletcher and Son, Swalwell, 1964.

Emmerson, John. *1st Whickham (St Mary's) Scout Group History 1915-1985*. Published by the Group, 1985.

Focus Magazine. Various articles on aspects of local history, published by Whickham U.D.C., 1966 to 1974.

Fordyce. *History of Durham*, 1857.

Gladstone, W.E. and the Revd R. Corker. *A Short History of Dunston and St Nicholas' Church*. Warwickshire Publishing Co. Ltd., Birmingham, 1965.

Gould, Revd W. *Speculum Gregis*. Manuscript, 1853.

Lambert, Charles. Various booklets on aspects of Whickham history. Undated.

Lewis, M.J.T. *Early Wooden Railways*. Routledge and Kegan Paul, London, 1970.

Lumley, D. *Echoes of Other Days: Some Leaves of Northern Lore*. Northumberland Press Limited, Newcastle upon Tyne, 1930.

Mackenzie. *History of Durham*, 1834.

Manders, F.W.D. *A History of Gateshead*. Gateshead Corporation, 1973.

Manns, Ernest. *Carrying Coals to Dunston*. The Oakwood Press, Usk, Monmouthshire, 2000.

Members of the Whickham Local History Class and their Tutor. Some Chapters in the *History of Whickham*, Co. Durham, 1961.

National Trust, *Gibside Chapel*, undated.

Newman, F.G. and Sunniside and District History Society. *Byermoor, Marley Hill and Sunniside*. Chalford Publishing Limited, Stroud, 1997.

Newman, F.G. and Sunniside and District History Society. *The Turnpike Road: Sunniside, Marley Hill, Byermoor*. The People's History, Seaham Grange, Co. Durham, 1998.

Nicholson, Isa. *A Short History of Swalwell and its Co-operative Society*. CWS Printing Works, Pelaw-on-Tyne, 1914.

Rix, Thelma. *St Mary's, Dockendale*. Published by the church, 1988.

Robinson, Ian. *From Abberwick to Yetlington: The Place-Names of North-East England*. G.P. Electronic Services, Durham City, 1999.

Thompson, Edwin. *The Story of Spoor Memorial Methodist Church*, Whickham. Published by the church, 1971

Thompson, Edwin. *Whickham West End Methodist Church*. Published by the church, 1969.

Whickham Journal. Various articles from *Whickham Journal*, published by Whickham and District Local History Society, 1976 to 1986.

Whickham Magazine. Various articles from the Parish Magazine of the Parish Church of St Mary the Virgin, Whickham.

Index